JAMES HOGAN

THE ART UPSTART

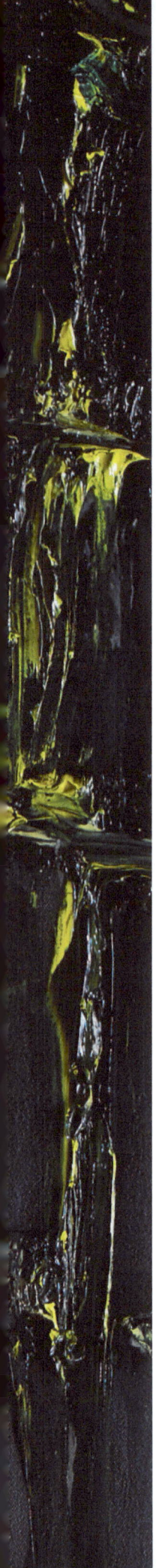

Published in 2014 by
The Edge Press

First published in
Great Britain in 2010 by
Goodsteed

A CIP Catalogue of this book is available from
the British Library

ISBN: 978-0-692-26884-1

Photograph Copyright © 2010
Vibeke Dahl
Justin de Deney
Jane Kinnock

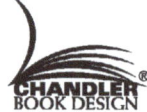

Designed and typeset by
www.chandlerbookdesign.co.uk

Paperback layout by
www.tomnorwood.com

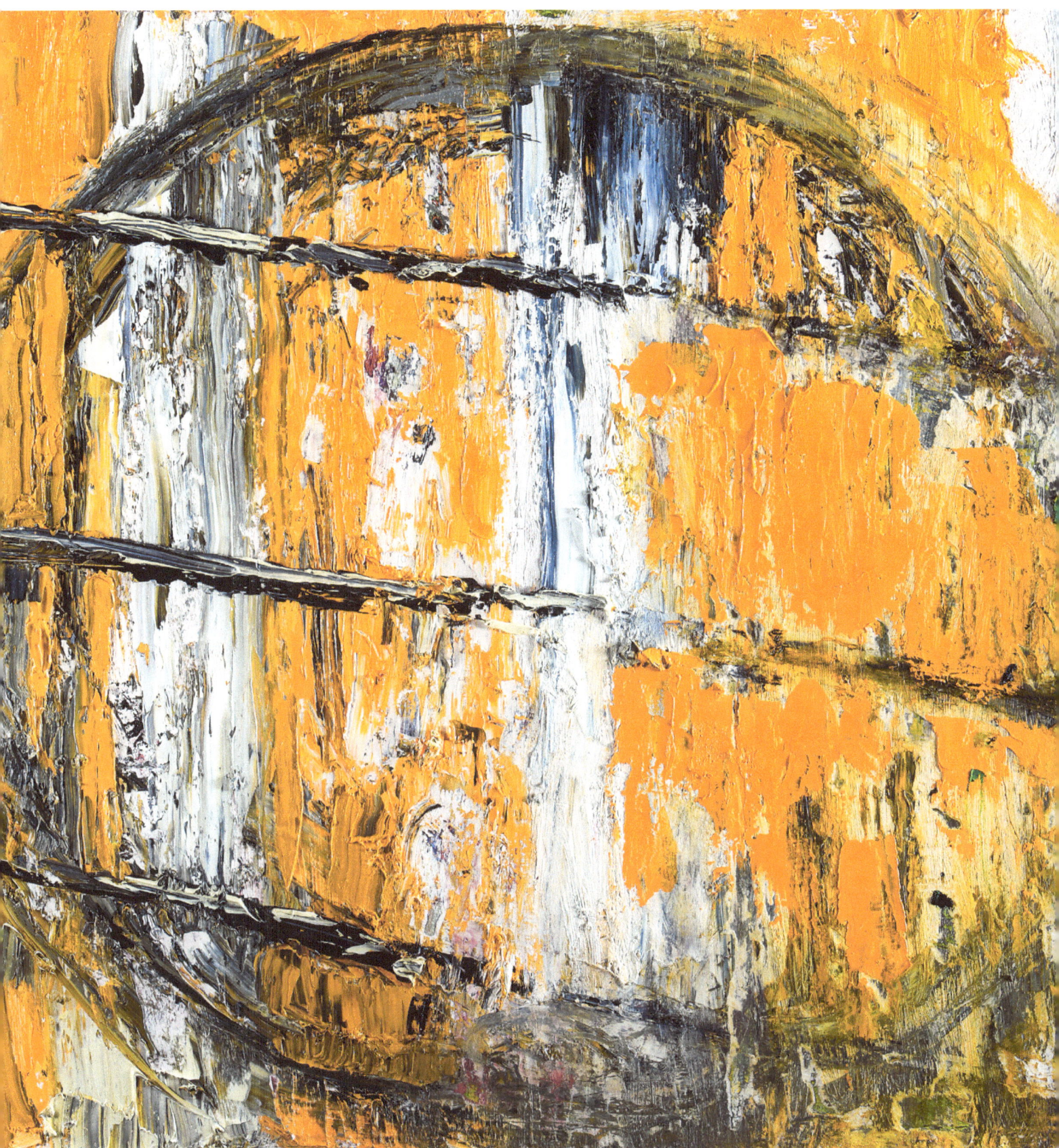

UNITED II *2008*

BLOOD V *2010*

ACKNOWLEDGEMENTS

I could not have written this book or got to the exhibition without the help, love and encouragement of my closest friends. Especial thanks to my wife, Jane, who has lived through every step of the process and provided me with total loyalty and support. She has not only put up with my obsession and the mess, she has acted as the project manager providing brilliant photography, advice about the paintings and the composition and setting of the book. Especial thanks also go to my dear friend and great supporter, Charles Denton. He has encouraged and inspired me every step of the way. Never doubting. Never giving up. He too gave me invaluable advice about the paintings and structure of the book. I owe him a very great deal. Especial thanks must also go to another dear friend and source of inspiration, Richard Glynn. It is thanks to Richard that I was able to see a way through at a stage where I was beginning to wonder whether I could pull it off.

I am greatly indebted to Claire Bailey-Coombs whose endorsement means so much. I also owe a great deal to Simon Packer and Sieng Van Tran who guided me through the digital side of the equation and advised me about how to build the website. I was also blessed to have several very brilliant interns working with me. Their youthful energy and sheer brilliance was inspiring. They are: Sarah de Haas, who made a huge contribution, Alessandra Durand, Tasnia Wahid, David Mitchell and Ahmed Ashraf. Ahmed is a gifted human being; I owe him a lot. At different steps they kept me going, always supportive and encouraging. My son, Alexander deserves a special mention also: he was meticulous in typing up and helping to compose the manuscript and helping me with breaking out the blogs from the long form. Thanks also to Philip Gomm, a fine writer who read the manuscript and gave me very valuable advice. Last, but by no means least, Alan Smith who has been with the project team from the start. Framing. Filming. Always kind. Always patient.

CONTENTS

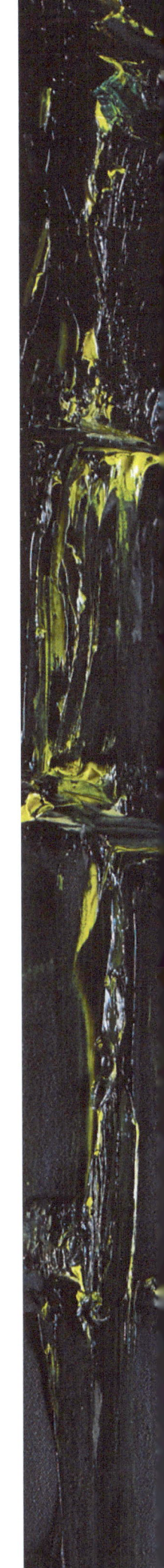

FOREWORD

by Claire Bailey-Coombs

Upstart *n. & a.* **(Person) who has risen suddenly from humble position; (person) who assumes arrogant tone.**

James Hogan, the Art Upstart. A man whose paintings are quite literally the expression of everything he is.

When James asked me to look at his paintings he wanted me to be brutally honest. The sort of request that usually makes me slightly nervous. But my reaction to them was immediate and very positive. I loved their very 'abstractedness'. I responded to the colours; the combination of the Cornish whites, blues and blacks; the deep blood red and ochre; and the joyous yellows and oranges. I wanted to explore the deep gouges in the paint surface (still wet in places) and follow the peaks of impasto and feel the gritty sand embedded in the paint (brought up from the beach in a bucket!). In his studio are piles of paint tubes, Kings blue deep, each one squeezed violently and distorted, testament to the energy with which he approaches each painting.

The images are at the same time both inherently simple and intensely complex. The basic shapes of circles, triangles and intersecting lines are composed of many layers and depths. The paintings have a commanding presence when viewed across a room or at the end of a corridor but must also be seen in detail, close up, to witness the sheer joy of the paint.

Some of the paintings are undoubtedly challenging, complex, even nightmarish and frightening, and definitely not for the faint-hearted, but their place is crucial when seen within the greater framework. They make the joyous ones even more uplifting and optimistic.

For James they are full of meaning, deep from his own experiences, and the process of painting them has been cathartic, paralleled with the writing of the book. The words and images tell the story. It is a herculean task; the full plan is 225 paintings, each one a stepping stone, a landmark or a mile stone. And all this from someone who has had no traditional art training and who looks to no other artist for inspiration or influence.

But one feels compelled to draw comparisons. The intensity and sheer volume of paint brings to mind the work of Frank Auerbach and Leon Kossoff, and there are similarities in technique; the use of palette knife and the scraping-back of the paint before loading it on again, building layer after layer. The subject matter has parallels with Paul Feiler; the swirling circle exploring space, tone and light.

James seems to put a little bit of himself into every painting. He has a very driven impulse, a need to create. There are no preparatory sketches or drawings, the paint is worked straight onto the canvas with a palette knife, scraped back and reapplied, wet-on-wet, the colours mixed on the canvas. He uses broad, gestural slabs of colour, often threatening to leave the canvas and spill on to the frame. The image in his head is so strong that the transfer from mind to canvas is direct and immediate. The result is one of incredible impact and strength. Each painting has a vibrant energy which demands attention. I defy anyone to stay silent in front of any of them. They inspire comment.

James is not a follower; he has charted his own artistic course, approaching his subjects in a way that lets the viewer see the world in a new light. His work takes courage, the paintings are emotionally charged, and at times it has been a painful process – echoed in the very physical nature of the painting process. His paintings, like him, are flamboyant, brilliant and passionate. He is the Art Upstart.

THE START

went back to painting at the beginning of 2007 because I had to. When I woke up at the start of the New Year I felt a tremendous urge to work with colour and light, to touch the paint, to feel the canvas, to use the knives – not brushes, knives. I don't know what triggered this but it was as compelling as the sexual drive of youth. I was hungry for it. And I have been ever since. It is a biological need that once more has to be satisfied. I think that one of the things that happened was that my love for ideas had been reflected in the written word ever since I was thirteen, to the exclusion of paint. But I had always been able to paint. It is not difficult for me. So I guess I stored up all the images in my head as I went about my life. And that they simply had to burst out at some stage. Of course, I had to be ready. I had to be sufficiently confident about who I am in order to do it – to risk. But the sheer drive to it do it overcame any fear of rejection. Today paint is as big a thing in my life as 'God'– not least because it is so near to 'God' – a source of light and meaning that exists in the same way that a beautiful flower exists. The hero in my work is 'God.' Not the religion of God but the God of religion.

Strangely, the impulse to paint has increased the amount I write – not diminished it. I would never have written this book were it not for the desire to set my paintings in context. I want people to understand what I am trying to say. What the shapes mean, the concepts behind them and how they fit into my life story. So words and pictures go hand in hand. They help each other. The paintings have also allowed me to psychoanalyse myself. A difficult process. I know myself a great deal better today than I did three years ago. They have helped me to fill in the missing years. By going back and recreating some of the images from my childhood, painting has helped to heal my soul. To fill a bit of the void, to take away some of the spiritual loneliness I felt following the death of my father and then my mother. My mother really died when he died. So they were one and the same event. 'Paint' helps, 'God' helps.

When I picked up the knife I had no idea what to expect. I went to the London Graphic centre in Shelton Street in Convent Garden and bought up lots of materials. Took them home, laid them out, and started. As I used to do as a child, albeit in watercolour then, I put on the oil very thickly. I did not want to be taught by anyone. I knew they would just get in the way. I did not want anyone to come between me and getting the images out. I will always feel that. Layering on the paint I knew why I was attracted to the knife – thickness. I also discovered that my style of painting would be best suited 'wet on wet.' The combination of manipulating the knife over wet painting layered on wet paint was magical in its effect. I could trap the light. I could mix and match very thick lines with very thin ones. One of the things about oil painting is that every picture is totally unique. No two oil paintings anywhere in the world are the same. I found this idea very exciting. Exhilarating. Entrancing.

My paintings depict the interaction of life-experience, history, and philosophy. At one level the paintings illustrate the way I see the world having evolved – the way we all experience certain aspects or live out certain philosophies. The way the world has been revealed to us. Hence, the empathetic phase in which there is no distinction, between subject and object, followed by creeping distanciation and objectification. Followed by the impact of the dialectic, anomic, and alienated forms. Juxtaposed is God, 'Christ'. Hence the eternal struggle between good and evil. This dynamic is explored in the later series in the first 75 paintings entitled **'Eclipse'** and **'Blood'.** On another level, my work reflects my own experience of the world, growing up, sadness and joy, struggle and a revealed truth. From the time I started to paint again these two tracks or stories seemed to overlap and fit together. Perhaps that is inevitable. It is certainly true that they were both there from the start and that they drove me to a definite style straight away.

I painted the story in a very linear way – but at first the pictures took the lead. Later the words took over for a time. Then the emphasis switched back to the visual, reverting once more to words when I decided to write my life story in order to explain and support the paintings. The words also took me by the hand, just as the paintings did. After I had painted about a dozen pictures, I started to fill out the written story – at first on just four pages that I pasted into the front of my portfolio. This allowed me to stand back a bit, to consider what I was doing and why. It also gave me a roadmap for all the paintings that were to follow. I could see all 225 – the first 75 very clearly and in great intricate detail. The remainder more sketchy, but definite. It also showed me the gaps. I could see some of the missing images from my childhood. So I decided to recreate them, using minus numbers so: -1,-2,-3 etc. The words had taken me over the 75 mark for the first chapter. I did not want to break the symmetry so I removed some repeated images and replaced them with three minus numbers which would be counted within the 75. This book covers the first chapter of the story – the first 75 paintings.

So to the story : **'Genesis'** is what you would expect – the start of it all. This is the first oil painting I did.

I wanted to represent the beginning, however, in a very modern, visual way – almost 'televisual' and certainly very graphic. The use of the re-worked, multi-layered colours, bright greens, yellows, and oranges was to signal eruption, the bursting forth of life, of unrestrained energy, the triumph of nature. Impactful. Hopeful. The colours used in **'Genesis'** are also intended to lead to the use of the rainbow in **'Empathy'** and at different stages of the work. At this early stage I used the brush and the knife.

'Empathy' reflects the undifferentiated, pantheistic state of man's existence in which subject and object are wholly integrated. There is no looking out, only looking in. Man and nature are one and the colours harmonious. The circle is used to reflect this because it is a complete form that is never broken. The full range of colours from the rainbow is deployed. The lines of the circle embrace man. Nothing jars. Everything is whole. The pantheistic image is conveyed through the use of multi-layered paint – thick and thin – which casts its own shadow as the paintings are viewed in different lights throughout the day. The overall impression is of being inward-looking. There is no observational perspective. Your eye is taken into the centre and only travels out to the inner ring of the circle. The use of thick white titanium encircles the imagery, further circumventing the overall impression and meaning. 'Empathy' also denotes the earliest stages of my life when I was closest to my mother's bosom – my world a world of warmth, of security, of certainty. There were no outside forces. No disjuncture. Nothing broken. Harmonious. Unchallenged. I probably lived in **'Empathy'** a lot longer than most of my peers.

My upbringing was typically inner-oriented as an immigrant. My mother didn't like the English – as a generalisation. She didn't like moving around society. Her focus

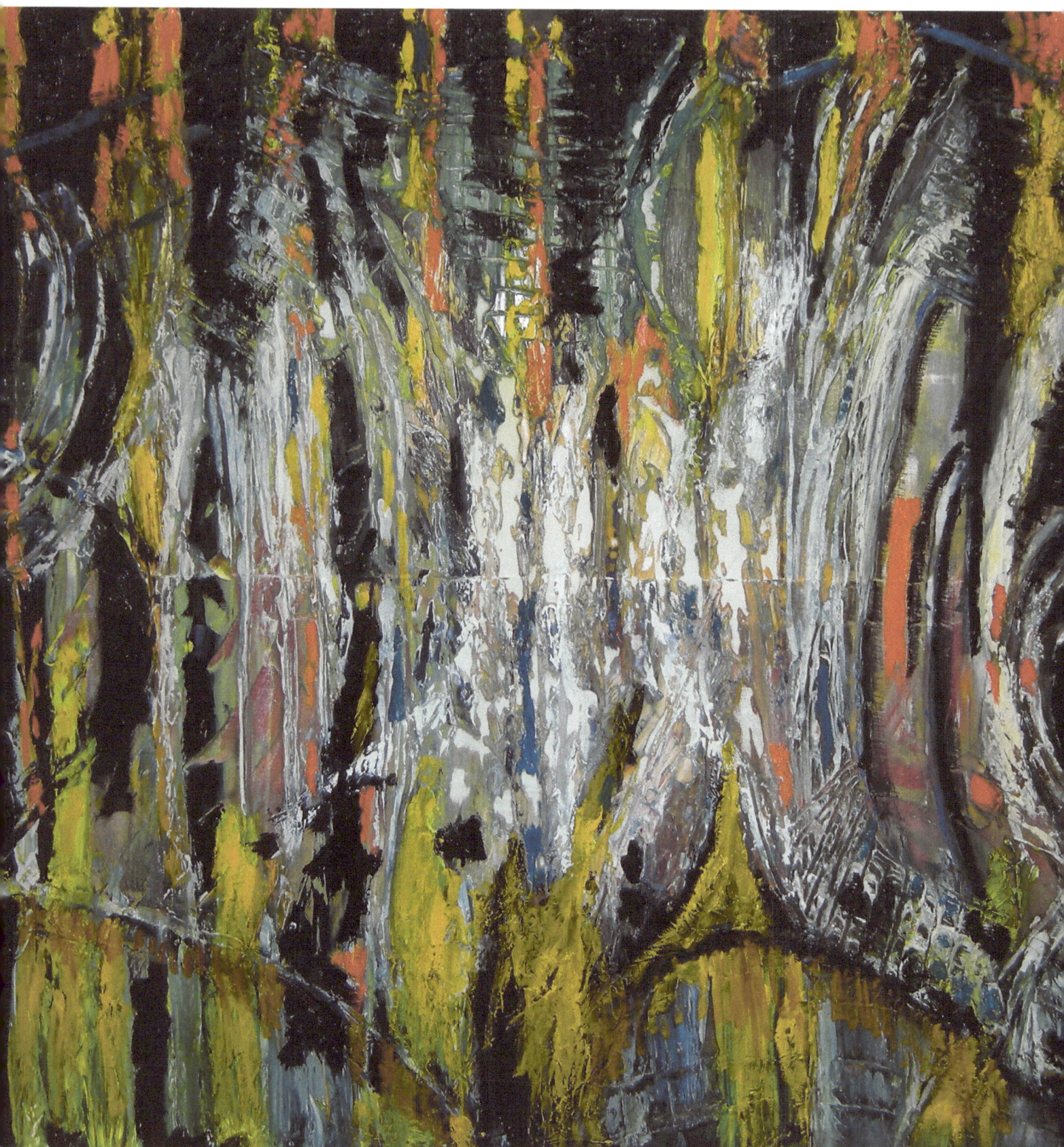

GENESIS *2007*

was my father and us as children. When we walked down the street she would cling to me as much as I would cling to her. This could have perverse consequences. I did not want to leave the surety of my mother's love – I saw no reason to go to school. In the event, I went very late. Dogs seemed to symbolise the threat, the aggression, of the exterior world to my mother, and therefore to me. She was terrified of them. To her the world was a threatening place – when she was taken out of our home. In my mind **'Empathy'** reflects the state of consciousness that existed inside our house. By the time I was seven years old my mother and I had to make the outer journey to **'Optic.'**

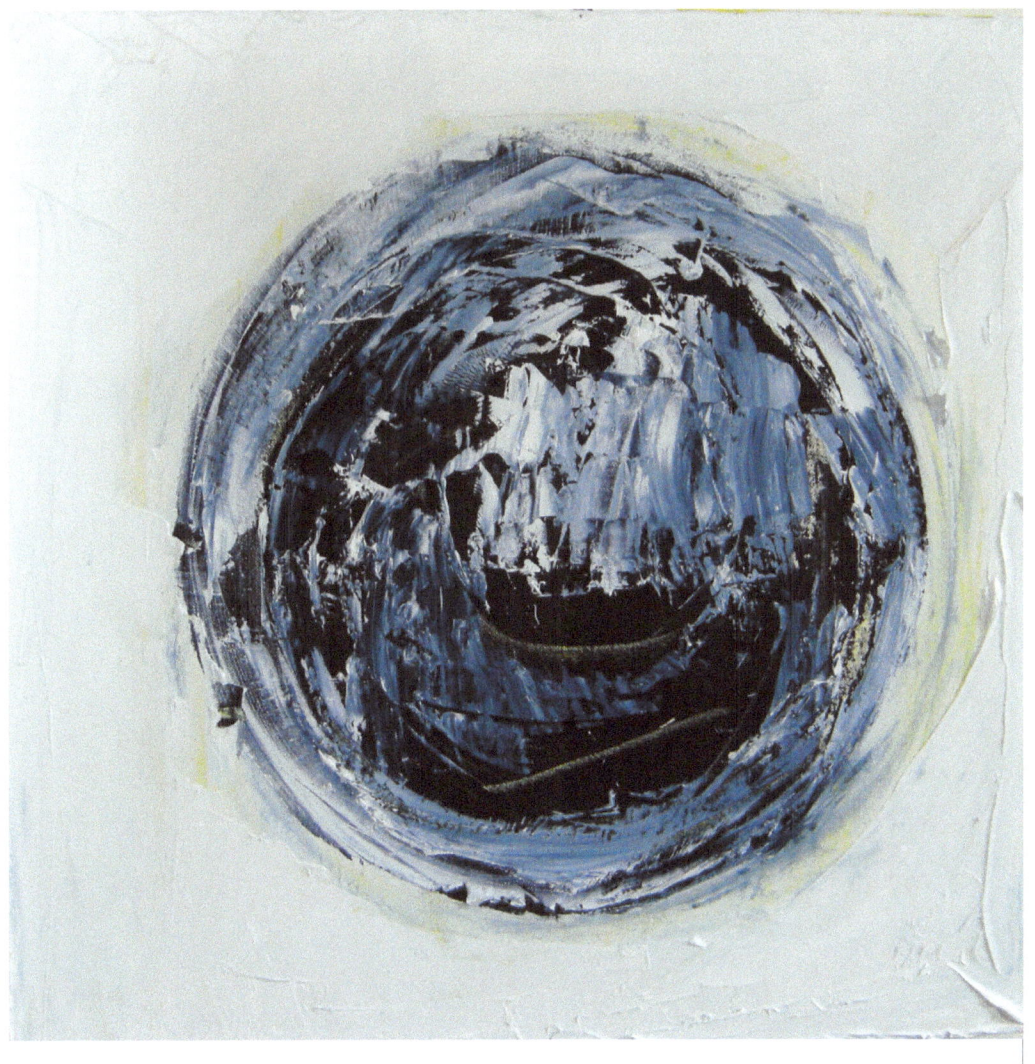

EMPATHY VI *2007*

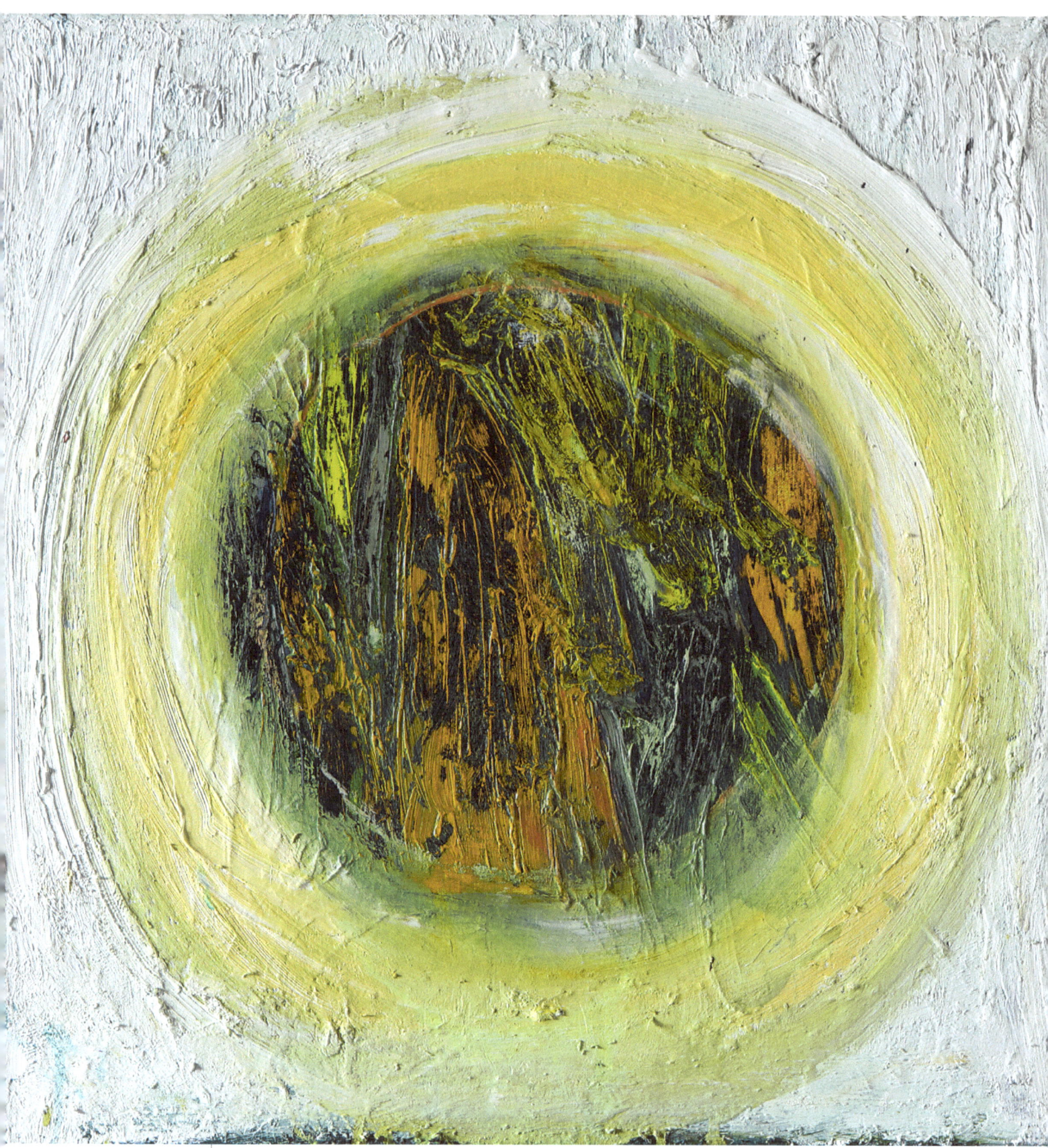

OPTIC III *2007*

'**Optic**' reflects the next step in the development of human consciousness – the looking out, beyond, to the dawning of a subjective being. With '**Optic**' the perspective shown in 'Empathy' is reversed. Instead of looking in, looking out. There are three '**Optics**' to reflect the right and left eye of man – and the spirituality or promise of a 'third' eye. To this extent '**Optic**' is a pre-echo of Christ which represents not only good but total perspective – the origin of being, historiography, cosmology and so on. The order of the optics is also important when viewed in this way – first the blue – the sea and the stars, the globe – then the green of the land – both painted with a solidity, followed by the more refined lines and colours of the yellow optic – reflecting movement and a growing awareness of what is beyond. The '**optics**' also have a very direct and personal meaning for me. Because of my sight, I have always been obsessed with my eyes. As I started to grow up, from the age of five or so, I became acutely aware of my abstract eye. My left is very lazy. I cannot read with it. I only see shapes. So as I looked out I was very aware that something mechanical was happening. My right eye was 'empathetic' with the world; my left gave me a very insecure sense of moving outside of myself. The mix was very potent. Ironically it gave me a faster route to alternative ways of seeing compared with most people. Certainly that is always how it has always seemed to me. As a child, I repeatedly drew and painted pictures of the eye in which blocks of light illuminated the pupil. Like a lot of people my right eye was patched for a time – a procedure that proved useless because it was done too late. And I learnt to peep over and around the patch. The idea of patching the good eye was that the weaker left eye would work therefore and improve. I found this scary too. I really couldn't see without my right eye. In my case the effect was the reverse of what was intended. By peeping over the patch I actually started to use the good eye more – to look out, to start reflecting on my state of consciousness. The right eye was the '**Optic.**'

As a developmental stage you should say that human consciousness moves from the empathetic, to the optic, to somewhere between the two – to take stock. '**Reductio**' and '**Principia**' capture this state. There is a precision creeping in about cause and effect, about the parameters and contours that frame our understanding – but it is still at an early stage. These paintings reflect the tightening of perception. The harder lines. The heavier colouring. The arithmetic element points to the empirical method of the adult world – not yet present but coming. Even so things are settled. In my case this stage coincided with going to school. Learning to read. Accommodating the arrival of my younger brother. Up until the age of eight, I was only one of three children.

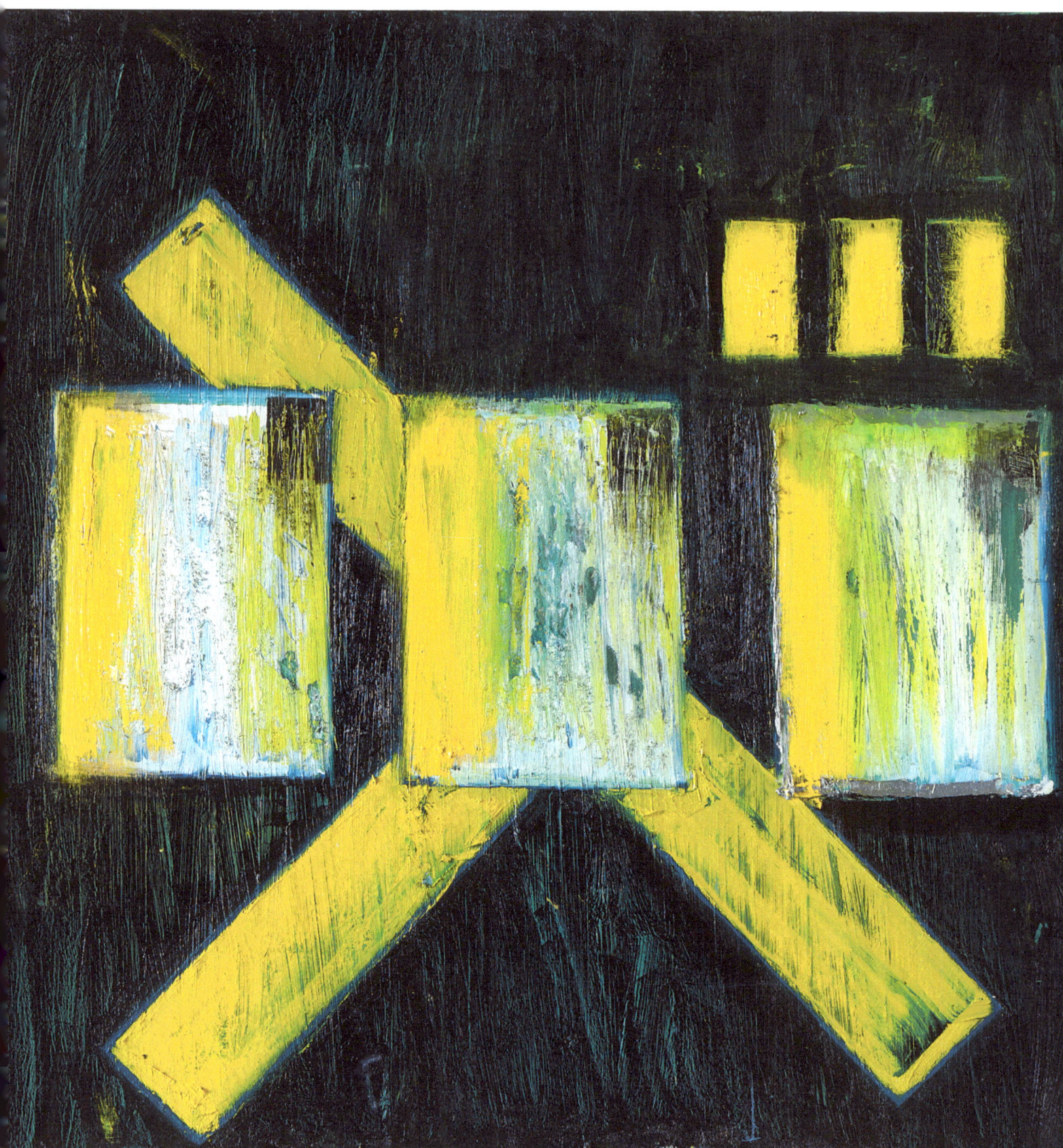

PRINCIPIA *2007*

This is important. The triangular could be given space. I could exist quite happily in this world. I had enough room to think and breathe. **'Principia'** with its three arms, three blocks, and three yellows, provides a visualisation of this pretty, happy state of bei ng.

At this stage 'Christ' takes over. The 'God' concept. It is no accident that the Jesuits knew when to introduce the idea of 'God' into man's consciousness and that time was early. 'God' makes most sense to the collective consciousness when that consciousness is still tender. Still being formed. As man looks beyond his immediate frame of reference – he is more open to the idea of a grand design. After all, children understand the idea of 'good' and 'evil', 'friends' and 'enemies'. Because they are dependent, vulnerable. They need succour and protection. They need something to hold on to. The notion of 'God' either as a living entity or as a concept is the most powerful idea in the world. One way or another all our thinking revolves around the proposition – be you a believer or an atheist. The 'God' concept is infinitely flexible, transmutable, and universal. It supersedes all cultures. In my paintings I use the word 'Christ' to represent 'God' when illustrating the collective consciousness and as a symbol of good. The Christ burns in man's perception of the world and anchors it. When I was painting, the Christ appeared from nowhere, with no warning. I just had to follow it. It took me to places I could not have foreseen. At first to the sheer representation of its power – the iconic abstracted images set against a holy blue – baby blue – Kings blue deep. Then on to the deconstructed Christ almost destroyed by modernity – but not quite. This is represented by the shattering of the stained glass Christ. We then enter the twentieth century and the head on clash between Christ and the evil of both fascist and communist ideology. The Christ is evident in the abstracted series **'Eclipse'** where various Christian symbols wrestle with the symbols of evil in different cultures, culminating in the deconstructed swastika over-laid with holy blue. **'Eclipse'** is about struggle. 'God' or 'Christ', it is about the never ending fight against evil and man's wickedness to man. In this series the Christian symbols of the flaming chalice: Ichthus, Chi-Rho, Latin Cross, and the Ark of Salvation are juxtaposed with the fasces; Hammer and Sickle and Red Star. In the Blood series Christ is threatened by Al Qaeda – but never defeated, never entirely absent. **'Blood'** illustrates man-made atrocity. More challenging is **'Hell,'** which denotes natural disaster – arguably the biggest threat to Christ, to belief in an omnipotent God.

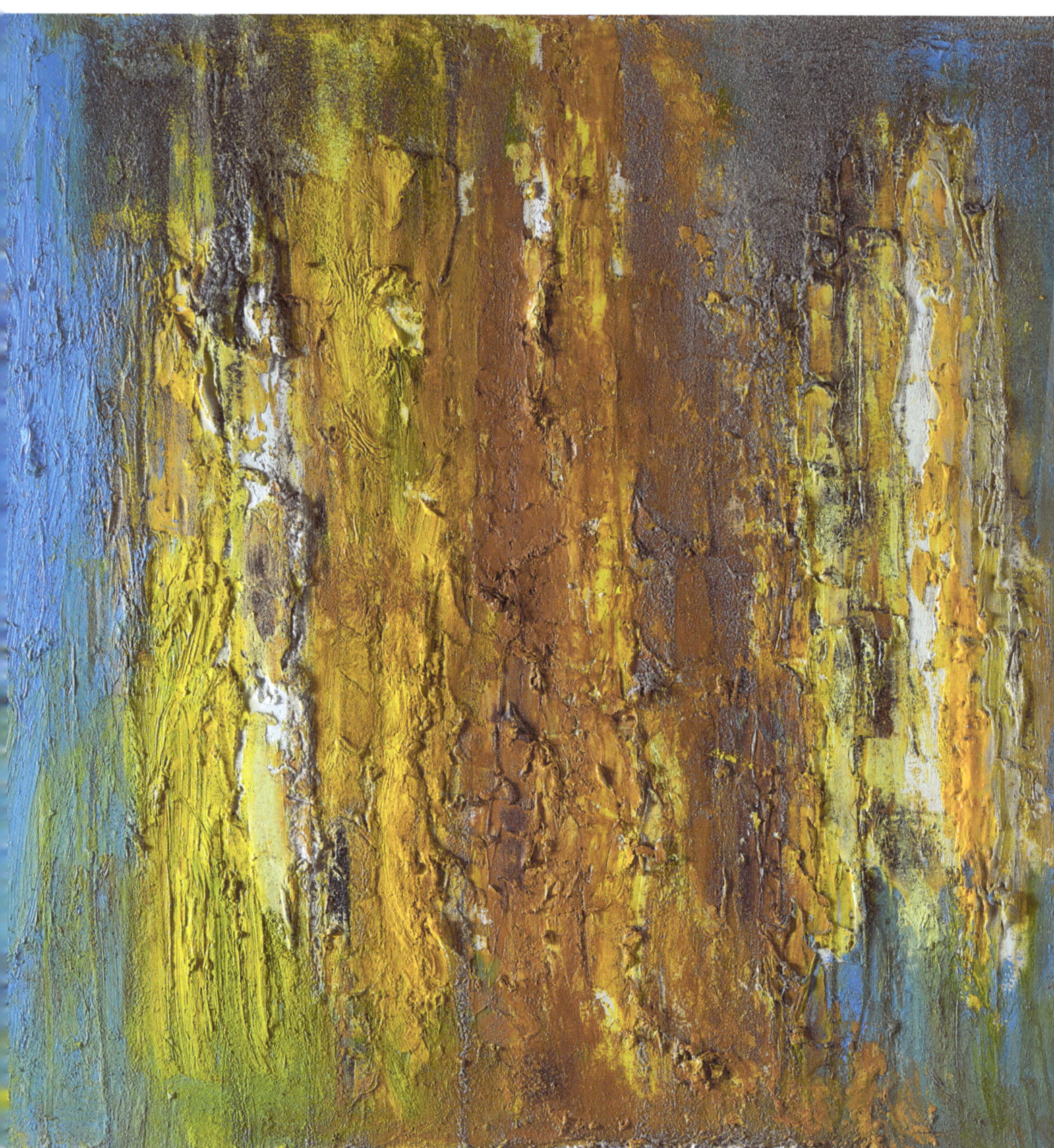

CHRIST V *2009*

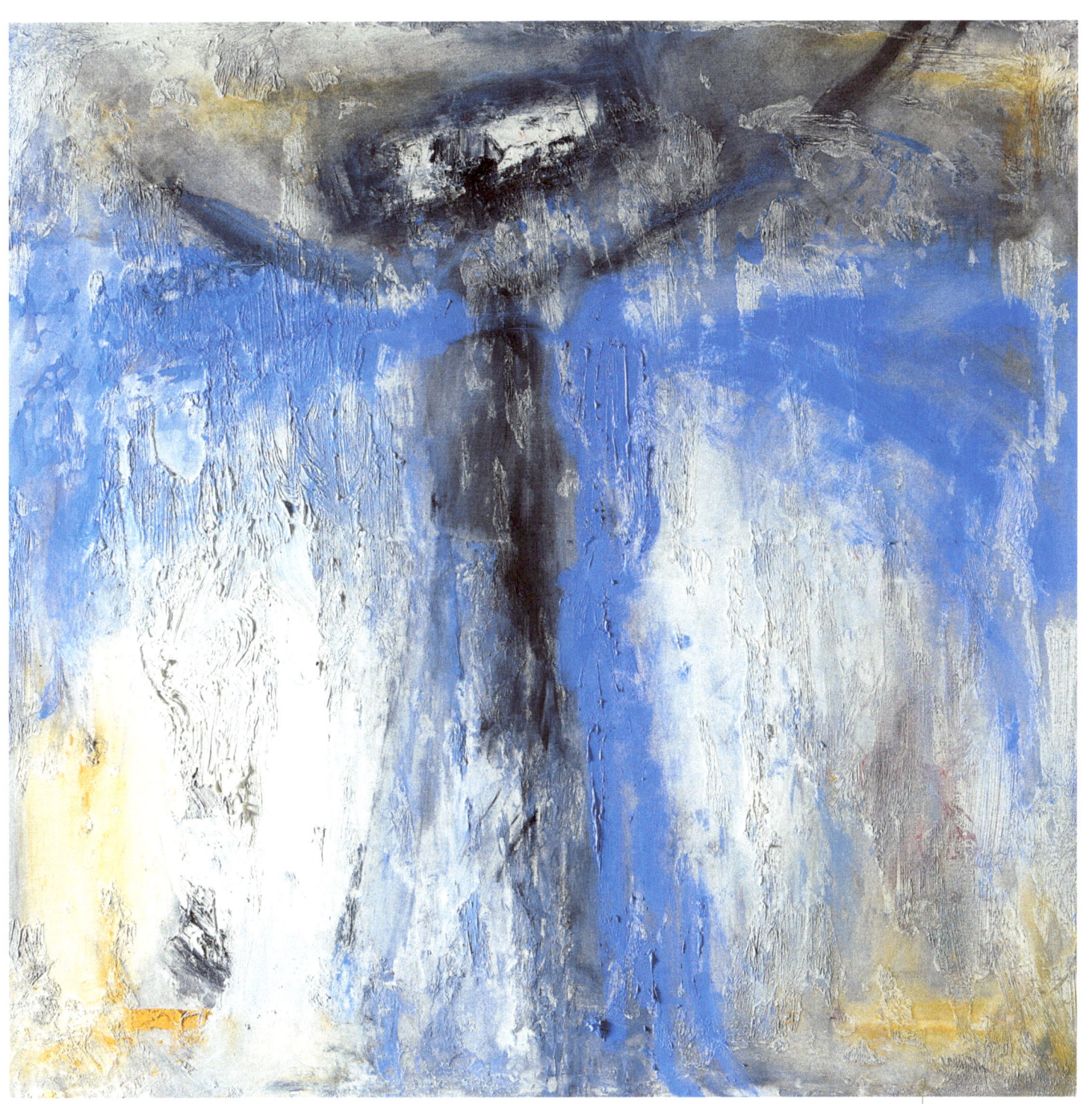

ECLIPSE IX *2009*

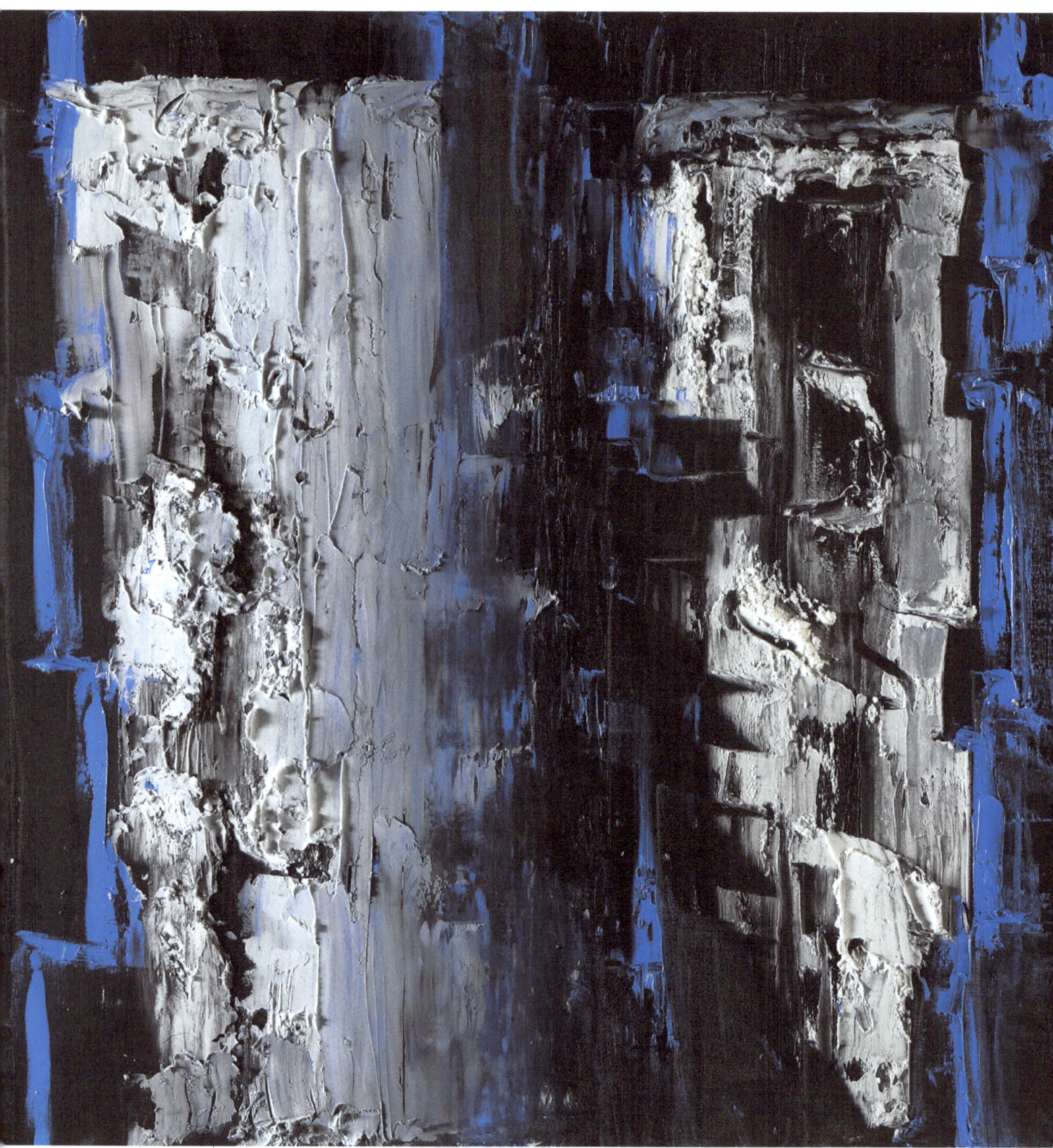

BLOOD IV *2010*

I use the word 'Christ' because of the way it captured my imagination as a child and because it is the greatest story of all time. The two biggest brands in the history of the world are 'Christ' and 'Nazi.' In my mind, the two have always been bitter enemies; the clash of their symbols is violent and potent. In my vision there are no cultural parallels. Of course there is good and evil, different religions, different codes and symbols. But the abstract imagery of 'Christ' and the 'Swastika' are the most potent of them all. Later on in my work I clash these head on when the chronology dictates it.

Beyond the 'Christ,' man becomes embroiled in a much more brutal reality – the **'dialectic'**. The **'dialectic'** frees man and imprisons him at the same time. It is a

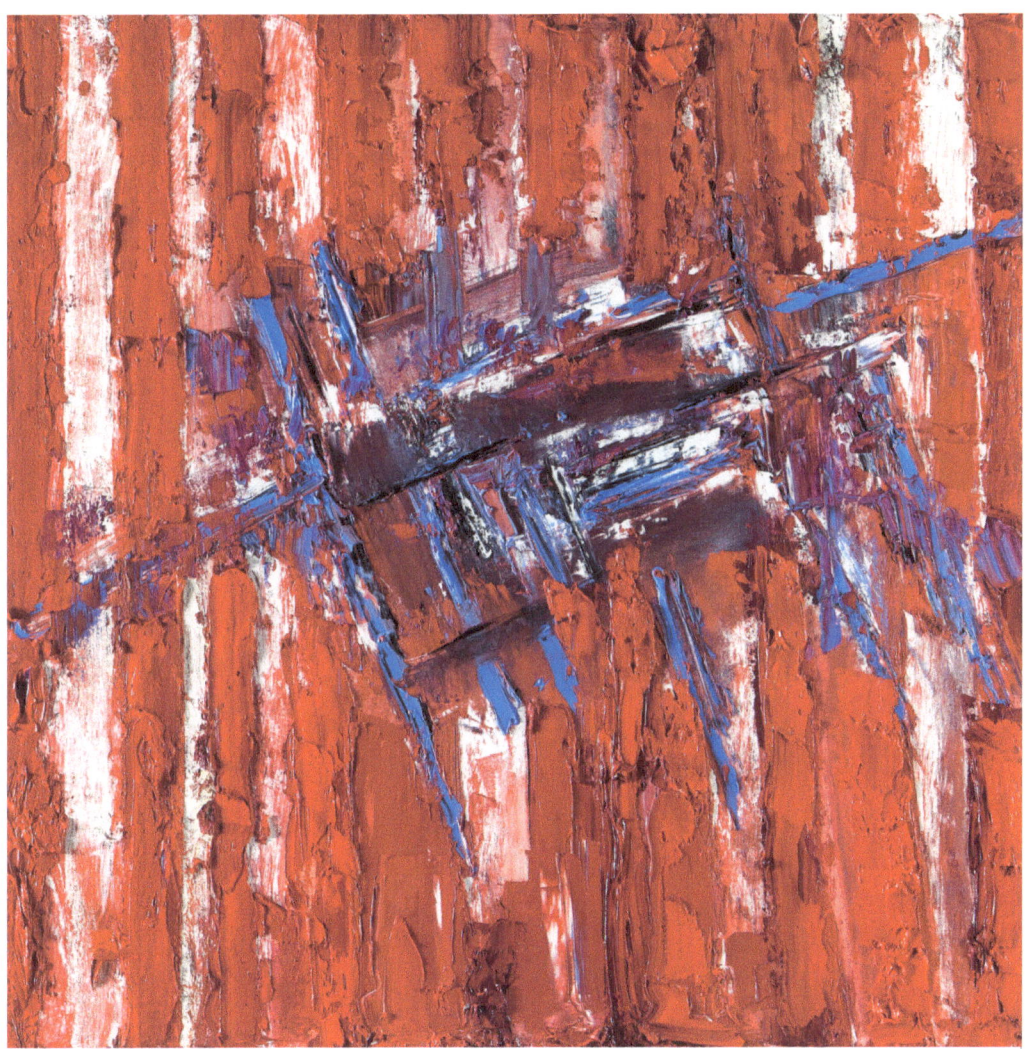

ECLIPSE VIII *2009*

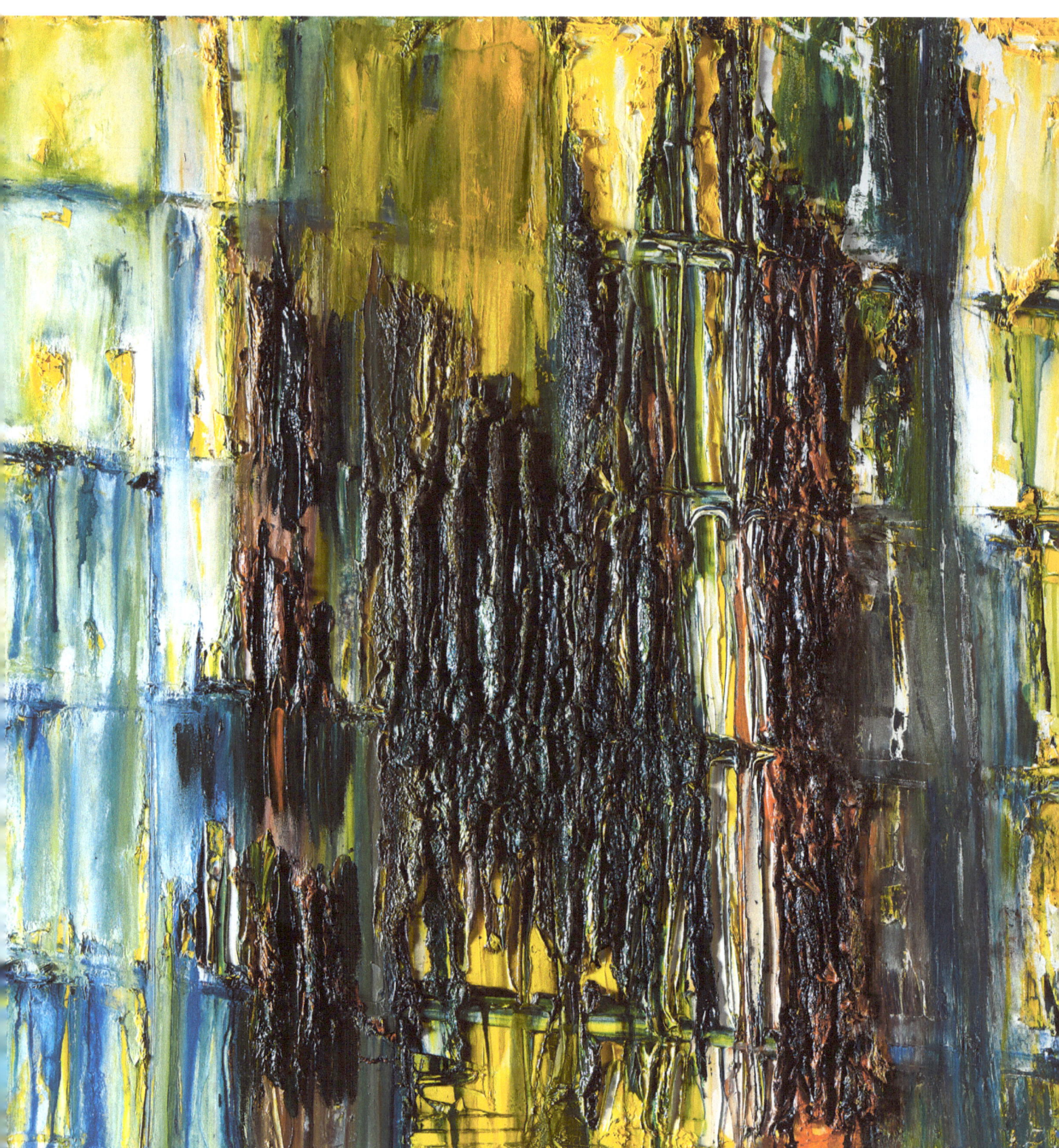

DIALECTIC IV *2007*

huge idea. Not as big as 'Christ,' yet it makes an enormous impact on the collective psyche. It is the science of Marx, Hegel and others. It is the process of making the emotional pseudo-scientific. It is the consciousness of industrialisation. In my painting, the power of the **'dialectic'** is illustrated in the strong lines, very thick paint, use of lacquer and yacht varnish to represent a way of seeing the world that pulls no punches. Economics determines behaviour. You do 'x', you get 'y.' No room for doubt, they believed. No room for experiment. 'Christ' would be redundant. No grey areas. No fuzzy lines. Hard reality.

The **'dialectic'** in my paintings is as powerful as I could make them. I used seven or eight different types of the same colour in variations of them. I also layered the paint in the thickest slices I had ever used. I did this to convey strength. The impact of the idea behind them. I also wanted them to be beautiful because there is a beauty to the perfectly formed concept as there is with a perfectly formed equation. Conceptually there is a lot right and a lot wrong with the **'dialectic',** but it is a major signpost in the development of the collective consciousness. No one can doubt that.

In parallel with the way I see the **'dialectic'** operating on the collective consciousness, is how it relates to my own experience. In my paintings it coincides with the death of my father and the hardship that followed. And the long climb out of despair. It is impossible to exaggerate the darkness that descended on my mother. Impossible to under-estimate the darkness that flowed into my head and heart. These depths are shown in the way that some of the **'dialectics'** draw your eye into dark corridors – black spaces and places. Yet there was always light – in some of the paintings a lot of light. The presence of God. I gave my mother hope. All of the **'dialectics'** are very spiritual. They convey hope, reflected in the variety of colours, different textures, and the way that the yacht varnish catches the light. Along with the darkness, light gives hope. More than any other, these paintings reflect the coming together of a very powerful – very hard – idea or reality that I entered overnight when my father died. Chronologically, I became aware of 'dialecticism' when I was in my teenage years. I read a lot of Marx as an undergraduate. I cannot be sure when I connected the **'dialectic'** to my father's death, but it was probably when I was about eighteen years old. Later on I would reflect a lot on some of these linkages when I was at Oxford. I stored them up. They had to come out one day.

In my recollection or interpretation of the collective consciousness, the concept of anomie comes next. Anomie to my mind is another word for atomisation.

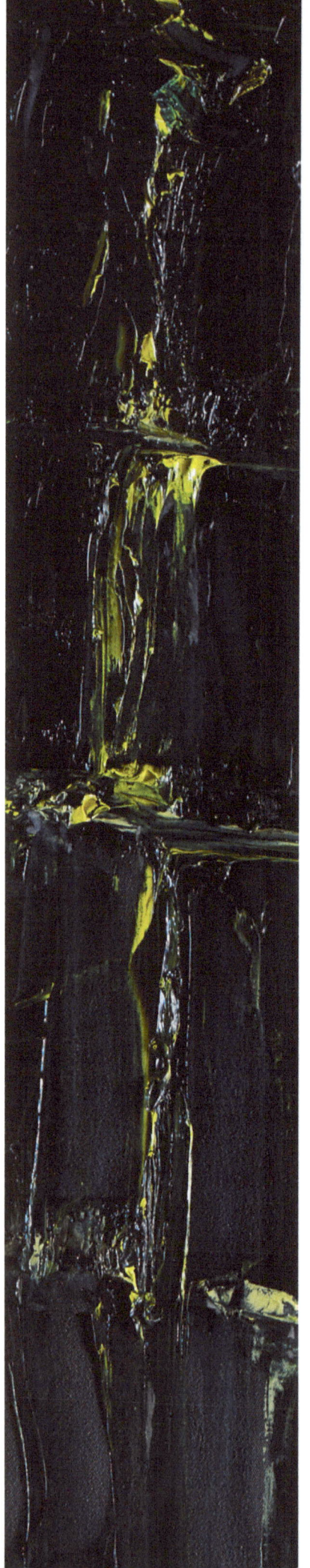

In the thinking of the great social scientist Max Weber, it describes the breakdown of community. However, that state gives rise to emotional feelings connected to a loss of space and identity. It is what happened in the run up to Nazi Germany, for example. The anomic consciousness – captured as '**Crucial**' in my paintings – is not a great place to be. Anchorless. All at sea. Yet even here to my way of thinking there are gains, anomie or 'crucial' accompanied a liberation of thought and feelings entrapped in the old order, including the **'dialectic'**. Anomie is a post-modern state, in which the individual is paramount. Left high and dry yet liberated. The paintings in this series explore various aspects of this – good and bad. There are dark patches. There are paintings where reality is left floating in mid-air. And there are the bridges from the **'dialectic'** to **Crucial** – the latter a corruption of the former to some extent and therefore quite similar except that the hallmark of **crucial** is a fluidity and looseness that is absent from the strident forms and certainty of the **'dialectic'** shape.

DIALECTIC V *2007 (detail)*

In my experience, **'Crucial'** matches the years after my mother's death. In this period I was truly free. However, I realised that in my case liberation meant having no one watching what I did.   Living like this is curiously exhilarating. But it is also cold and lonely. I lived in a heightened state of awareness in this period. I gained from that also. I acquired a sense of beauty. In both conditions – the **'dialectic'** and the' **anomic'** – you experience a sense of alienation, alienation from society, from self. This realisation is described in the series **'Strangers',** where the use of the triangle and the corruption of it and its lines reflect a feeling of marginality. In **'Strangers'** there are triangles within triangles. Lines within lines. Nothing is whole. Yet you can see what it should be like.

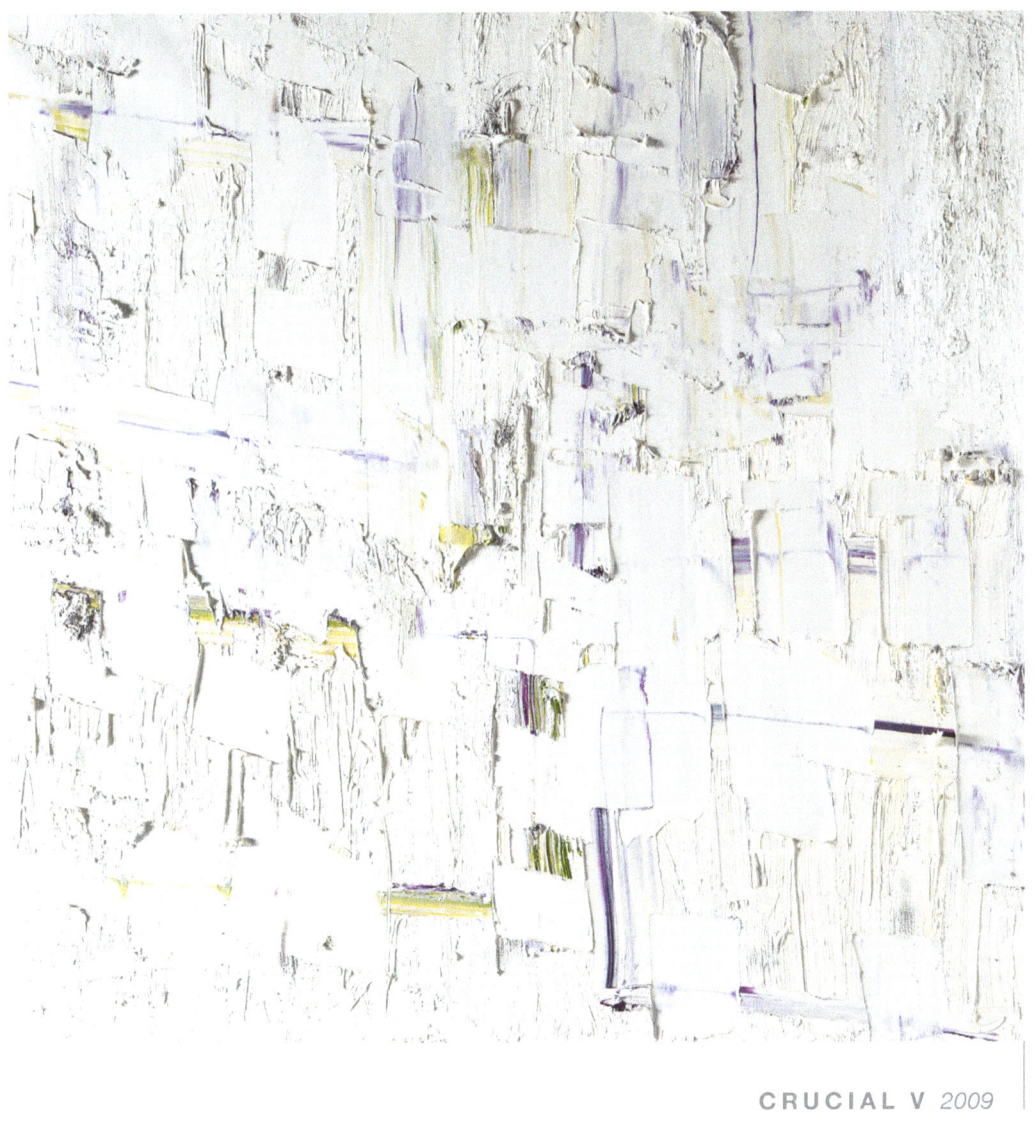

CRUCIAL V 2009

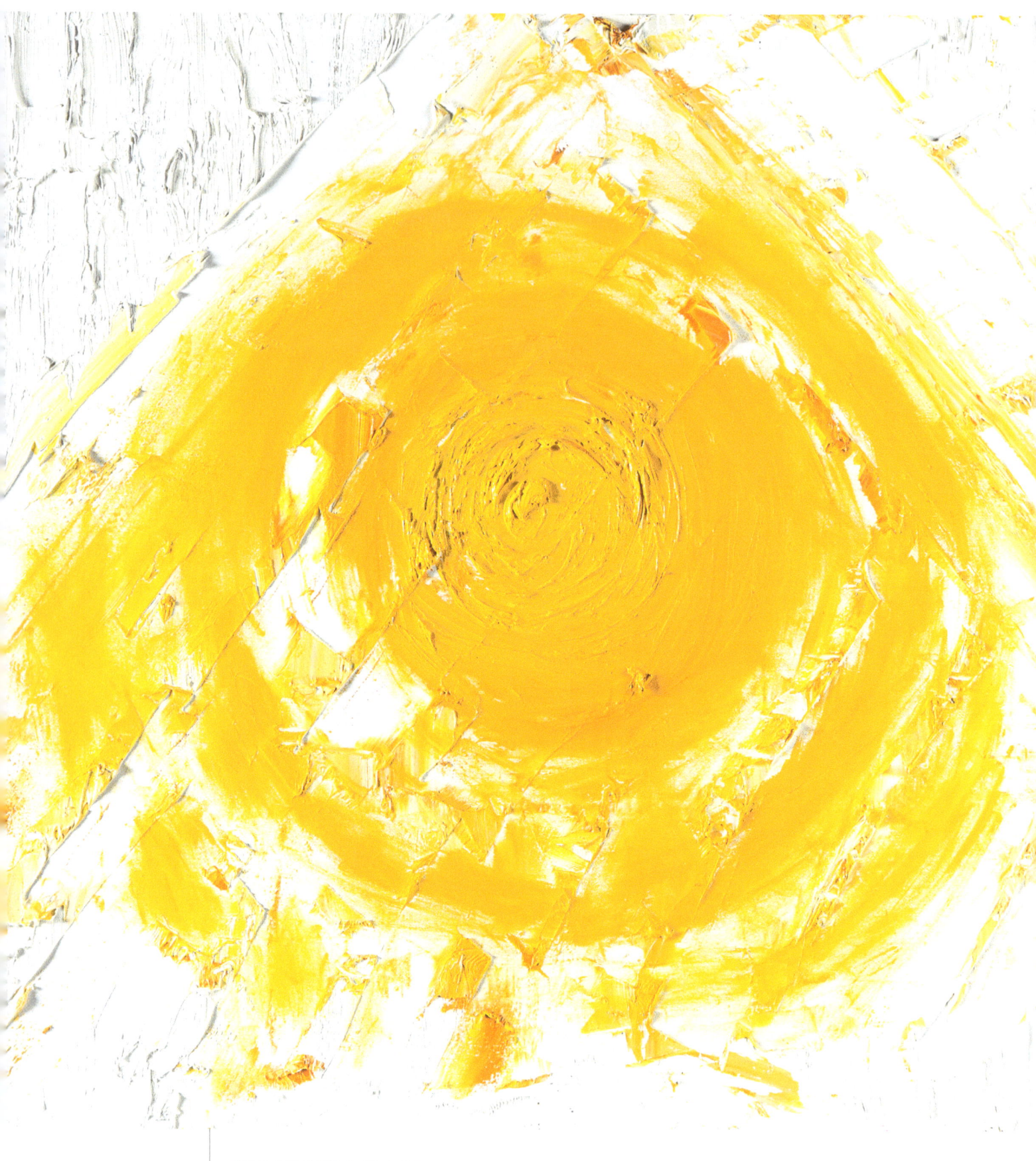

STRANGERS V *2009*

A healthy triangle. But you can also see where it breaks down. Where the connection between consciousness and 'fit' come apart. **'Strangers'** live on the edge and they are close to the edge. The beauty of the triangle even when corrupted points to a deeper meaning also. Hence the use of optimistic yellow. The self-awareness that is the ultimate trademark of the alienated consciousness brings with it its own blessings. You can see better. You can perceive more sharply. More accurately. I wanted to capture this by getting people to look once, twice, three times at the triangle because it was both beautiful and ugly in my conception. Because it is both clear and blurred at the same time. Revealing of consciousness and form.

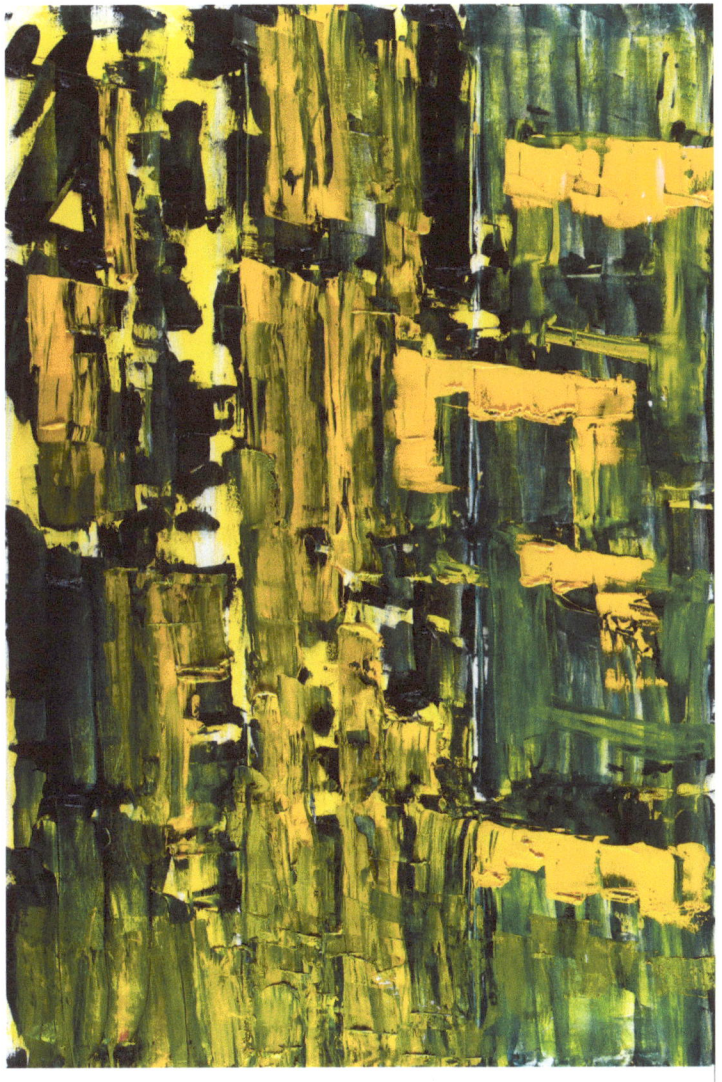

DILEMMA IV *2009*

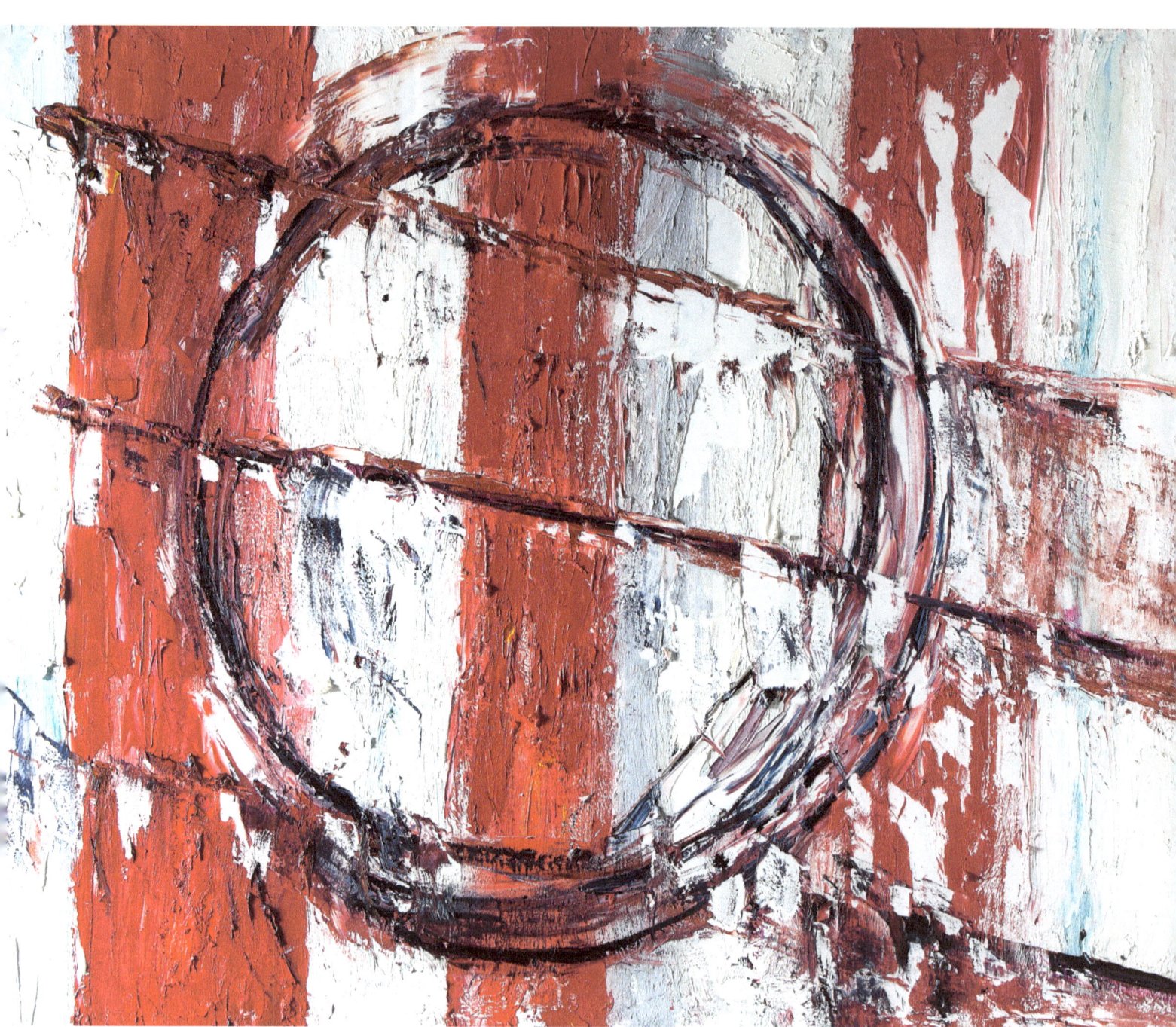

UNITED I *2008*

These paintings become literal when I stand back and analyse certain reference points in my life which intensified the feelings evoked here. The death of my father, for instance, gave rise to feelings of alienation from 'God' in my mother, as a result of which she felt very guilty until she died. I never doubted. Yet I am sure I absorbed my mother's awareness in my teenage years. School increased my feelings of marginality – even though I was good at the work. I was not typical. I was different. T his is the reason I never wanted to be taught art – or go to art school. Ironically, my independent spirit made me a very good leader. At this point I introduce Dilemma – As a punctuation point and a pointer to a deeper truth. There are four big panels – the biggest canvases I've ever painted. They pull together the three abstract forms that precede them and suggest an existential space to which they each refer and which we all inhabit.

A lot of my pain was taken away when I met and fell deeply in love with my wife, Jane. Jane is a very warm and loving person. We created a loving home together. Jane gave me security and confidence. Later we would have two beautiful children, a girl, Cassie, and a son, Alexander. The emotion that was released in me is represented in the **United** paintings in which the circle and the grid are intertwined.

The biggest influence on the collective consciousness in the modern age was undoubtedly the struggle between 'good' and 'evil' evidenced at its peak in the 1930s and 1940s, in which the distillation of evil represented by the concentration camps and Stalin's mass elimination of his own people – were to be a terrible pinnacle. While there has been ethnic meltdown across the centuries, the sheer scale and depth of the hatred and the systematic way that one section of humanity set out to totally degrade and destroy another puts this period into a unique class. The Nazi and Communist holocaust shattered the unity of the collective consciousness – the universality of the way that mankind thinks and acts. For all time thereafter we could never be sure of ourselves, never sure that it couldn't happen again. Never sure that some pool of evil inside of us would not well up at some stage to dehumanise our fellow human beings. Turning them into dogs. Treating them like dogs.

'Eclipse' seeks to reflect the struggle between 'good' and 'evil' that reached a climax in the 30s and 40s. And to carry backwards and forwards this theme. I chose the different symbols of the 'Christ' down the ages and juxtaposed them with the different

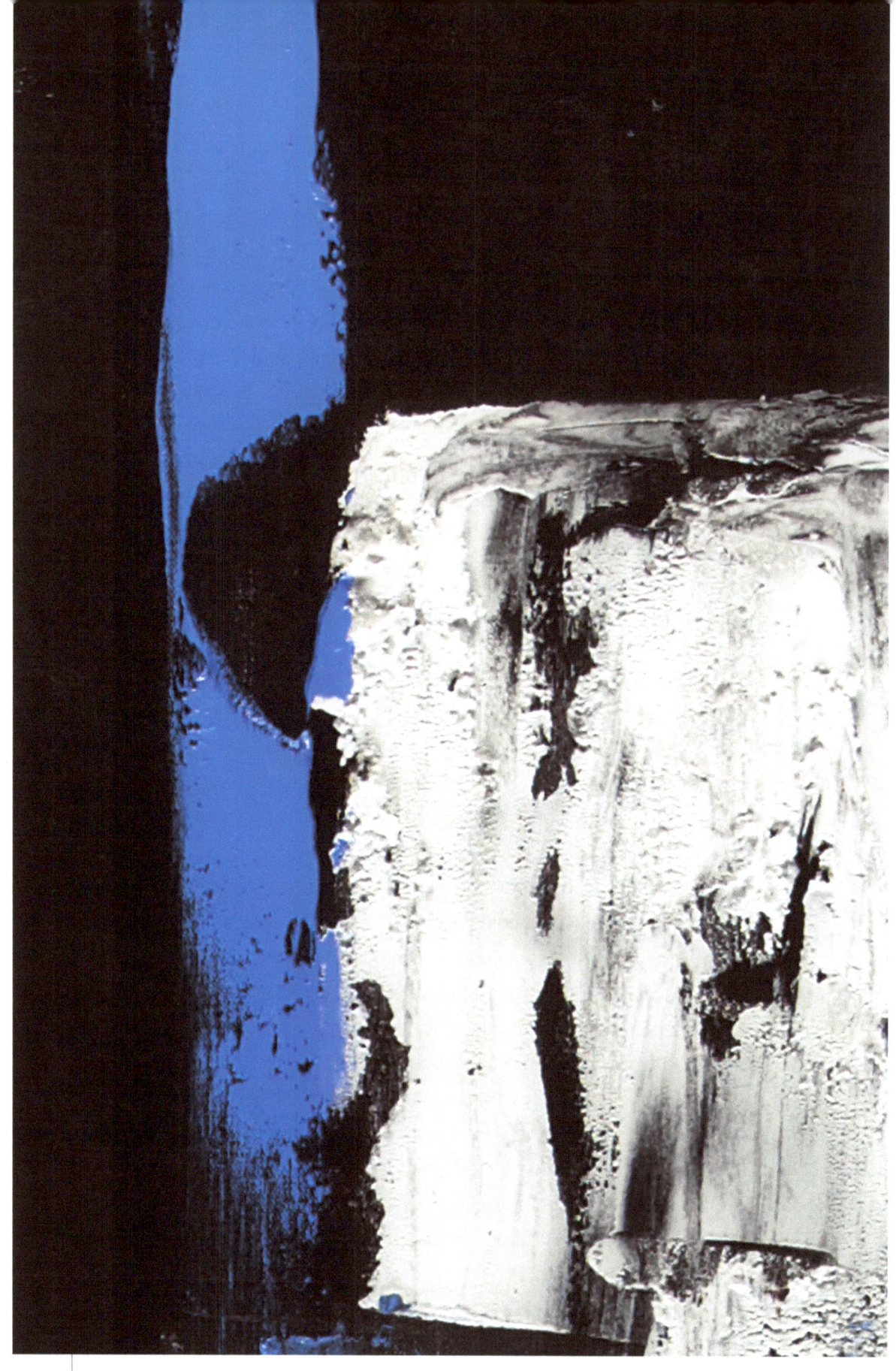

BLOOD III *2010 (detail)*

symbols of evil down the centuries. **'Eclipse'** is about struggle. The historic struggle for the battle between 'good' and 'evil' has always been with us. As with the earlier paintings, I wanted to deal with difficult subject matter in a visually appealing way. Partly, to gain an audience. Attention. Partly because even the most terrible events and episodes have beauty. I used the combination of titanium white, kings blue deep, the blue of 'Christ,' and amber yellow in these paintings because of the sympathy they evoke – this applies to paintings 1-7 in this particular series. The remaining three, 8-10, the paintings of the deconstructed swastika overlaid with the same blue, mark a more violent departure.

There is a terrible beauty in the emaciated bodies of the Holocaust. The beauty of the pitifully thin and battered body that refuses to give in or to give away its soul. Similarly in Hiroshima and Nagasaki. Later on, the four big panels entitled **'Blood'** explore 9/11, mixing the literal and symbolic, clashing the destruction of the twin towers with an abstract symbol of evil overlaid. Also the unresolved abstracted question – who is responsible for a disaster like Haiti?

The **'Eclipse'** series reflects events in my own life. I was brought up never to forget. The visit to the cinema to see the Nuremburg trials with my father when I was young was a seminal moment. So too was my Catholic upbringing. The Jesuit retreat. The hell fire sermons. I worked very hard at university and read a great deal. I studied Nazism, Stalinism, Mao, Terror. I went to the film club every week to watch the propaganda films of Hitler – Jews portrayed as vermin – stinking rats. I read about the dehumanising effect of ideological perversions. Psychopathology. Eugenics. As an adult, I am still transfixed by the history of Nazi Germany and the Stalin programs. I have watched endless television programmes about these. The images never cease to move me. I continue to bear witness. I find the two minute silence we observe on Remembrance Day – at 11 o'clock on the 11th day of the 11th month to mark the end of the second world war – very moving, as moving as when I was a young man. The struggle never ends. I have witnessed some terrible things in my life. They stay with you. But I have also witnessed great good – great acts of friendship and kindness. The two polar opposites feed into the consciousness of us all – as for me.

The series of paintings that follow on from **'Eclipse'** – **'void'** – are intended to capture, in abstract from, what happened to the collective consciousness after the Second World War. Here the unity and completeness of the circle is replaced by a set of broken lines and displaced images. The images are left hanging in mid-air to depict a sense of numbness. A lack of human feeling. After the eruption of violence and violent

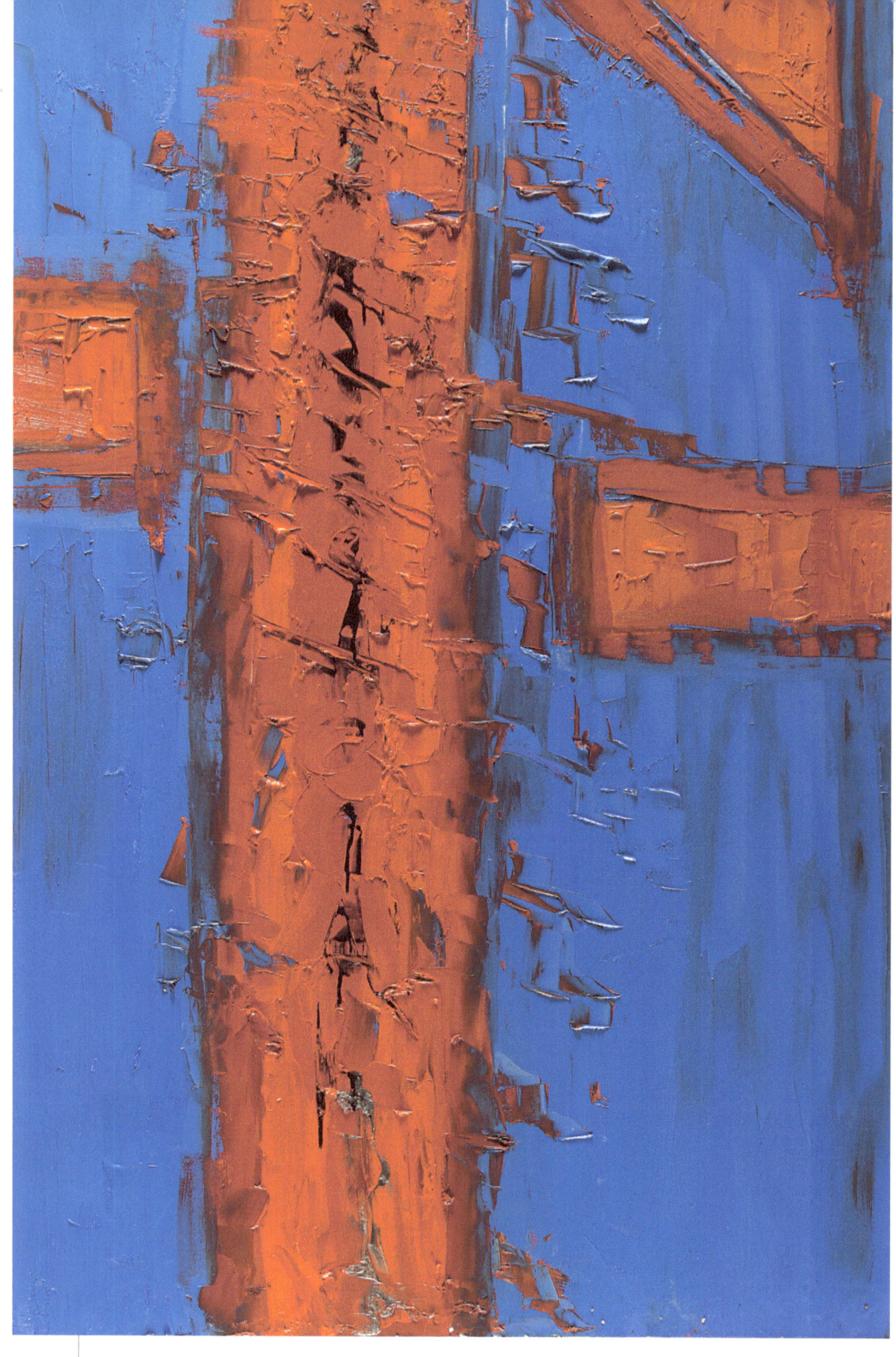

HELL I *2010*

emotion that preceded this stage there is a deathly calm. A disorientation. In a sense no-one can believe what happened. It is almost a mystery. There is the calm after the storm. A spookiness. Relief. But very little else. It is like the feeling after orgasm. All strength is sapped. For a moment, after the release, there is nowhere to go. You are just left lying there. You can't look either inwards or outwards – you just exist. In the history of emotions, not politics, that is what happened after the war. People licked their wounds. It took time to move on. In its way this period of **'Void'** is as important as any other. As real as any other. It couldn't have been any other way. Until the collective consciousness had gone through this period it was always going to be impossible to come out the other side.

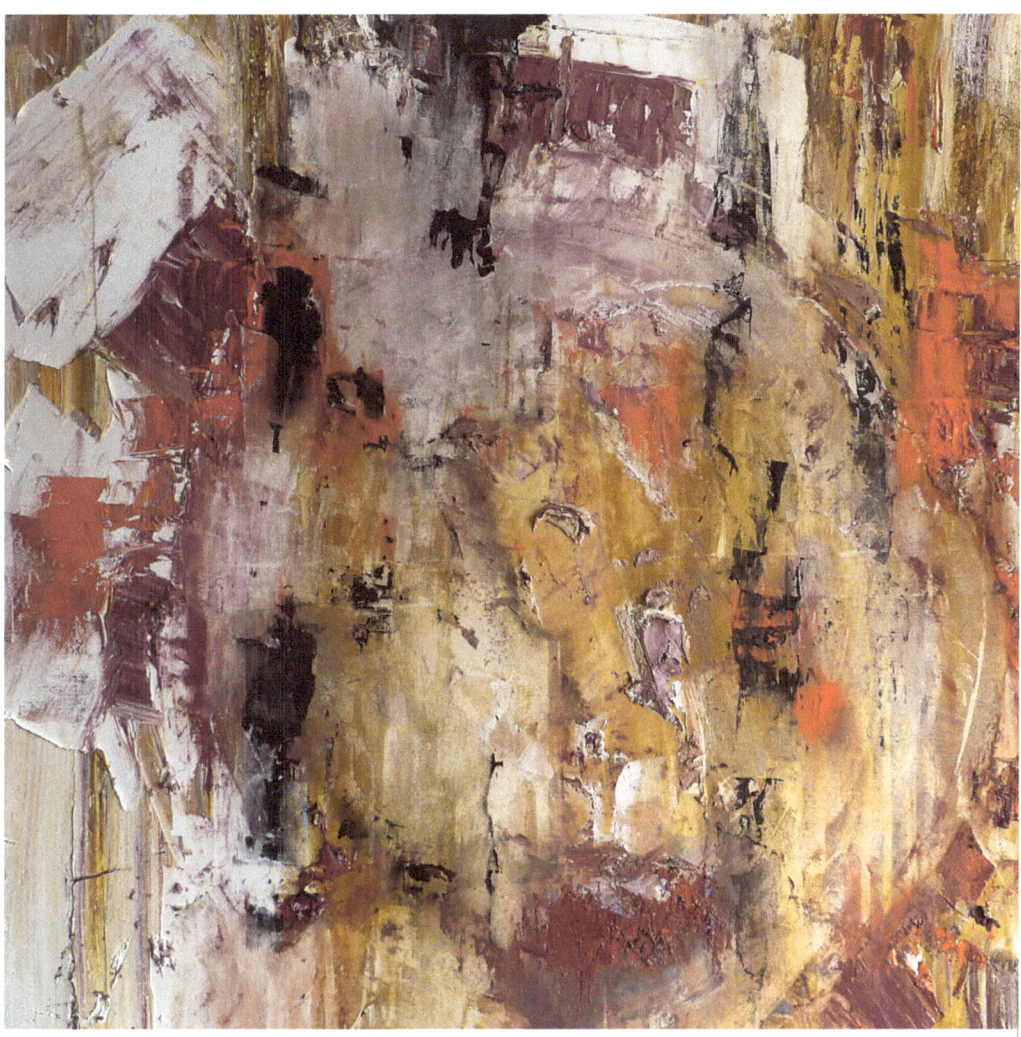

VOID I *2010*

The days and weeks after my mother's death equate to the **'Void'** in my life. Initially I wept a lot. Then I felt nothing. A total lack of sensation. I lost the power to feel. Very little moved me. I went back to university and lived alone. I could not have lived with anyone else. I did not have a sexual partner the entire time I was an undergraduate. I had anticipated my mother's death every hour of every day after my father died. I was always expecting it. Yet when it came, even for me, it was a dreadful shock. There was very little to be said about her passing in the end. She just stopped breathing. She just stopped being with us. It took me several years to move on. To heal. I learnt the meaning of being and nothingness. As in the paintings my strongest memory of this period in my life was the feeling of disconnection. The electricity of emotion had been switched off. Yet for all the pain it was a valuable – even very rich period in my life. I gradually learnt more about myself. That I needed to put the past behind me. Even put my mother behind me. And, to my amazement, I did not feel any guilt. It was over. Or it was just about to begin

The final steps in the story are, as always, a mix of good and bad. 'Blood' reflects our awareness that evil persists – threat. That there remains a lurking evil, a lurking terror, always waiting to erupt. That there is no security or certainty anymore – either physically or intellectually. Throughout it all, however, God never gives up. He is attacked. Diminished. Pushed to one side – from time to time. But he never leaves our side. He never left mine. The greatest challenge to belief is natural disaster. Not the hand of man. Possibly the hand of God. This poses a crisis of belief captured here in Hell.

The next book I will write describes and illustrates paintings 75-150 which explore the counter cultural influences in society that at first lay beneath the surface in the post-war period, only to explode in the late 50s and early 60s.

Book 3 will provide a visual abstract history of the three years prior to publication – as though a chronicle of world events is captured through the lens of an abstract camera in oils.

An emotional journey. When I started to paint again I had no idea that I was about to embark on an emotional journey. But I was. I was about to revisit my childhood and the upbringing that made me what I am. In particular I was to revisit the enormous love between my parents and my faith in God.

THE INDEPENDENT SPIRIT

There are two sides to every coin. Two sides to every personality. In my case, city PR man and artist. This is the story of the artist.

I was born on 12th September 1951 in Kingston-Upon-Thames, the second eldest child born to Irish Catholic working class parents – immigrants to the UK during the 1940s. They were to have six children. We lived in a three bedroom semi-detached Victorian villa in a place called Somerset Road – a happy *sounding* name.

My mother was born Bridget Lemon. She lived at 2 Olaf Street, close to the Cathedral in Waterford where grown men and women would routinely peel out of confession weeping, riddled with guilt and regret. Granny Lemon's house, two-up two-down, just, was always clean but reeked with the stench of damp. Similarly, my father's house in Barrack Street, Waterford.

My father was christened Thomas Joseph Hogan. Two good Catholic names. His mother, Anastasia, adored him. Poor, he was obliged to leave school at the age of fourteen. His father, Jim, was a cobbler by trade. My father, known as Tom, was an incredibly soft and sensitive human being. Then ugliness intruded itself into his life. He was sent to work at the abattoir in Waterford where the

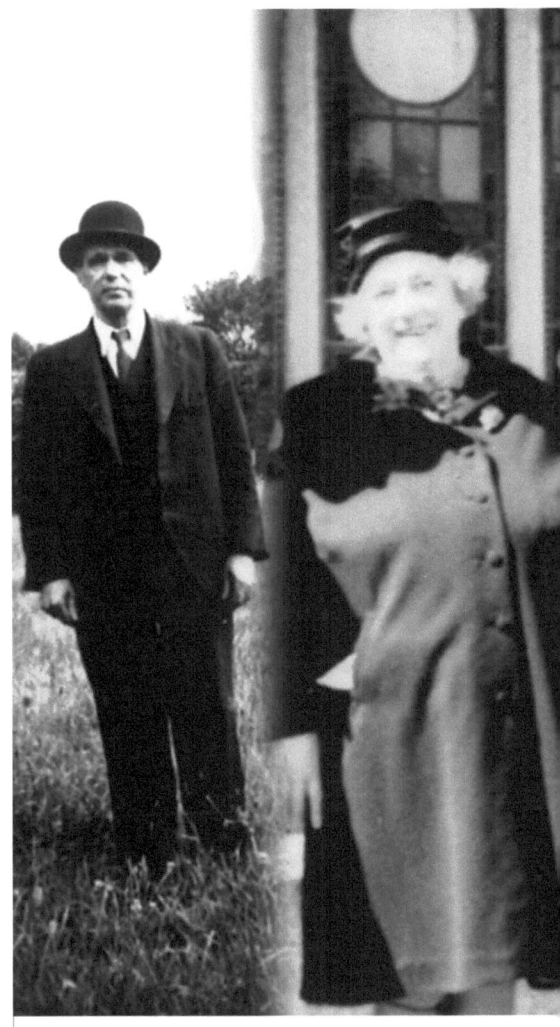

Grandpa & Grandma Lemon

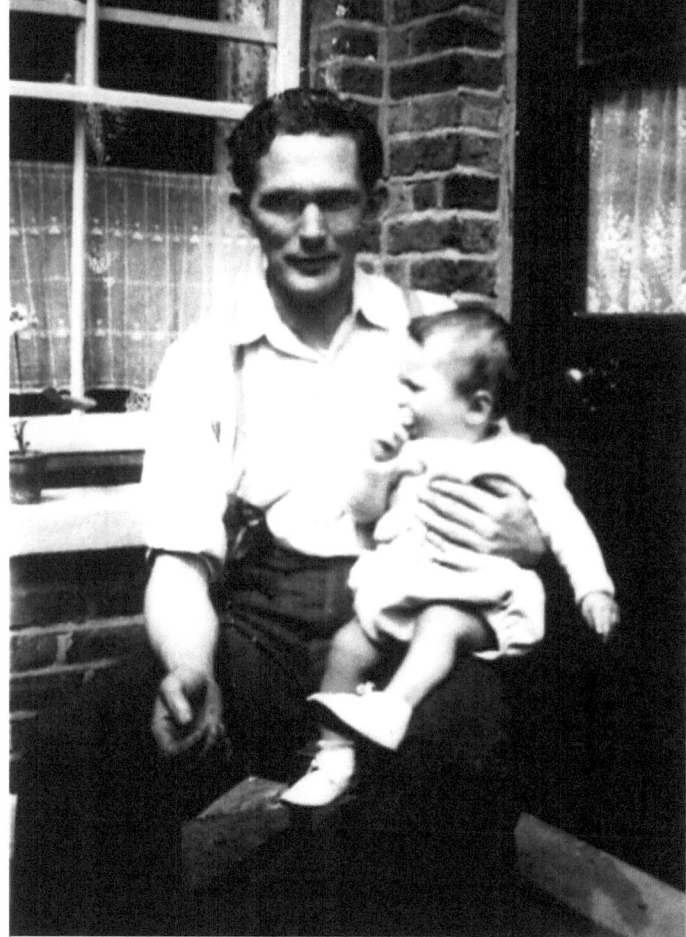

My father and me

blood of dead animals was tipped directly into the river.

One of my most vivid memories as a child was watching the thick blood flowing out of the factory, slowly diluting in colour as it caught the current.

For some reason, I always liked colour and light. My earliest memory is of being in the pushchair, pushed by my mother along the Fairfield in Kingston, with the spring blossom in piles at my feet. And later that day being parked outside the art shop in Kingston-upon-Thames, Surrey. And looking in the window at a box of oil paints in oak – which I could never afford. Of course, I didn't know anything about oils then, but I just remember liking the look of them. I think I sensed that paint would do something for me. I was immensely turned on by the different colours and by the chemicals surrounding them – linseed oil, turps etc. And I loved the knives.

After he moved to England in 1944, my father worked first as a painter and decorator, then as a factory fitter at Avery Hardle in Tolworth, makers of petrol pumps. Later he would become a shop steward. He was intelligent – an active trade unionist and interested in politics. He worked very long and arduous hours. He needed every penny he could earn to keep the family going.

When he left Ireland, his mother was devastated; she loved him as a son and

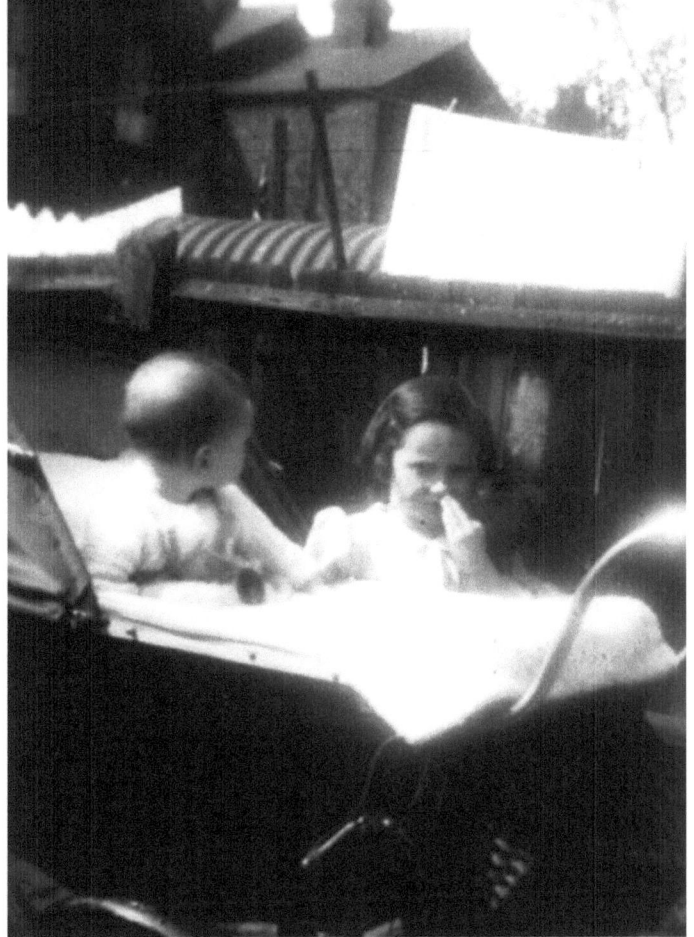

Me in my pram

as a leader. She looked up to him as a lot of Irish mothers do to their eldest son. When he wasn't working for our keep, he was constantly decorating the house, literally going from one room to another. Once he had done them all it was time to start again. There was no let up. I inherited his work ethic. Like him I never stop.

My parents were very Irish – not in a folksy way – but in their own way. They kept in close touch with Ireland, which they always called home. They read the *Waterford News*, which they had sent to them. Then there were the parcels. Specimens that would never be allowed these days. Gifts from home. A bundle of spare ribs. Sweating. Held together loosely by a bit of string, but delivered nonetheless. Or great lumps of shamrock, stuffed into little rectangular boxes. I remember going to school with what felt like half a tree hanging out of my lapel.

My parents loved each other very deeply. In addition, there was the anchor of the Catholic Church. They were devout Catholics. We all went to Catholic schools where we had religious instruction everyday of the week without fail. We always went to Church on Sundays and obeyed all holy days of obligation. We fasted and abstained when the Church calendar demanded it.

My parents had no doubt whatsoever that God existed or that Christ died on the cross to save humanity. There were bibles in the house, mass cards and pictures of the bleeding heart of Jesus pierced by a crown of thorns. When we visited Ireland – which I frequently did up to the age of thirteen – we would visit the houses of my grandparents in the City of Waterford, Southern Ireland, where at twelve noon we would kneel for the Angelis. As we knelt, hands clasped, we would stare up into the face of the picture of the risen Christ, behind whose head a golden halo of yellow shone. This imagery is reflected in my paintings, where I often set the blood of Christ against different sources of light.

Not only did my upbringing revolve around the Catholic Church, it also revolved around the drama of the Catholic year and ceremony. I remember vividly as a child fearing and loving the atmosphere that surrounded Good Friday where it seemed to me that it always became dark around 3p.m. The time that life drained away from the body of Christ. The stigmata painting of the dissected Christ evokes this memory.

My mother was certain about her faith. She knew God existed and was only too happy to believe that we were all protected because of that belief. She would say to me as a child that bad things never happen to Catholics or 'all good children go to heaven.' A phrase she used repeatedly.

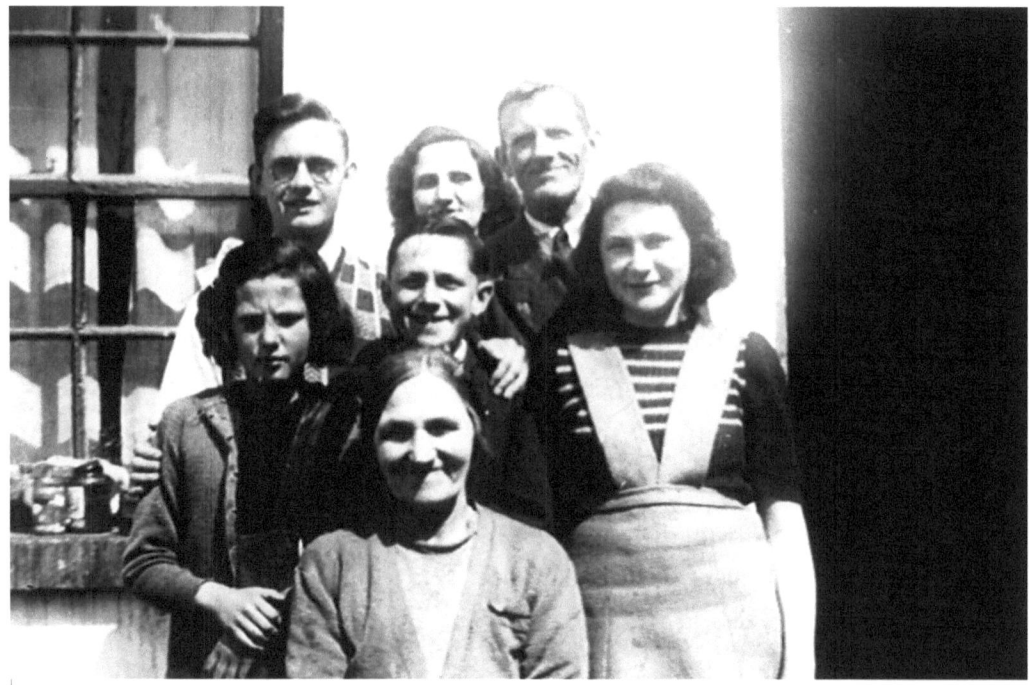

Grandma & Grandpa Hogan

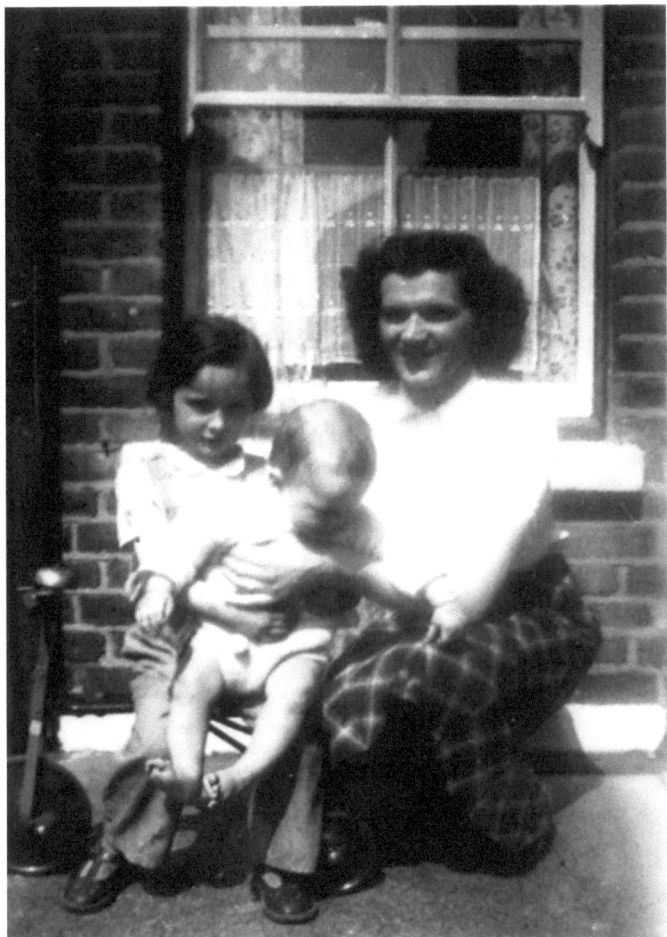

Me in my mother's arms

When we went to 'blanket street' – bed – we would always pray to God, thanking him for the day and invoking the good luck of the Irish and the Catholics. Their belief in God was more than a comfort blanket. It was the rock upon which everything else was built, alongside their love for one another.

I remember my first Holy Communion. The Easter light – new dawn. The colour of the host – off-white. The priest's wine. Blood red. I remember the texture of the host. The texture of the day. Thick. Overpowering. I fainted at the altar. I had been obliged to fast and abstain. I was overcome by the experience. I sat with my mother on the steps outside the church with Father Flood, a young, kindly and earnest priest. I recall the stained glass windows in the church – St Raphael's – deep purples, golden yellows, the echoed blue of Christ. This was to be my palette, and repeated through my work.

As a child, the church was home for me, within the womb, a source of solace and comfort. It instilled in me an instinctive response to beauty. And scale. It was by far the biggest and grandest place I experienced. Visiting it was like opening up a box of paints.

My parents' world almost exclusively revolved around their children and relatives, many of whom had followed them to the UK. Unable to afford to entertain friends or to run a car, we were hermetically sealed in a cultural bubble. We did not get a television of our own until the late 50s. This state of being is directly referenced in my paintings in the 'Empathy' series.

Inside the bubble a steady stream of relatives would arrive from Ireland including some great characters.

I remember my uncle Jack, one of my mother's brothers. He lived with Granny Lemon. I liked him, a lot. He loved gambling. Horses. Dogs. So did I. He took me to

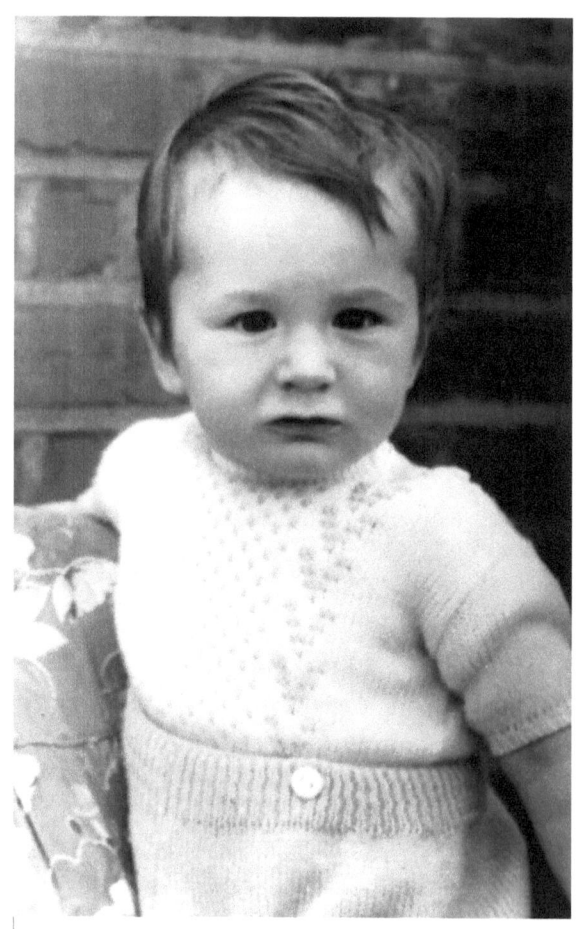

Me

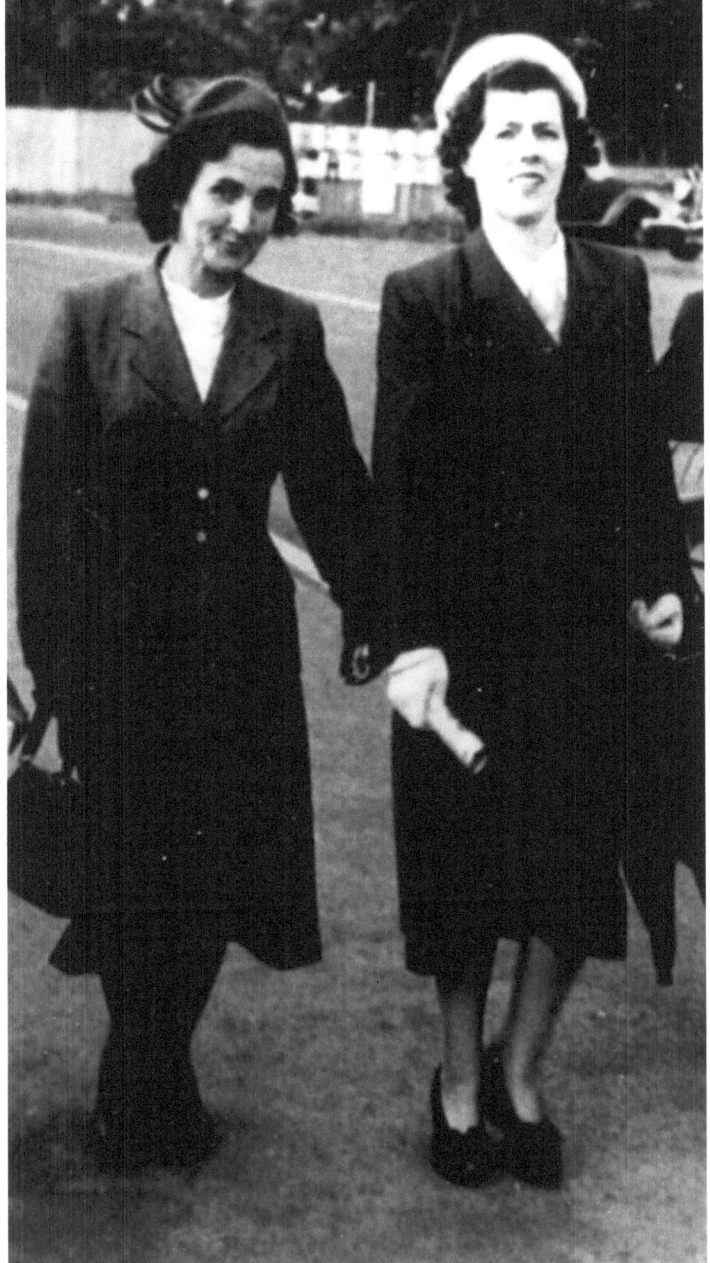

Nellie & Chrissie

the races. Together we would trip the light fantastic. At 5pm at the dogs in Tramore, beside the seaside, we would be full of hope for what might be: Picking a winner. Landing the big one. The colours. Tramore is by the sea – the sea and the stars. Blue. Green grass. Yellow sand. The different colours of the dogs themselves. Their skin. Once dogs start racing there is no stopping them. They fly past you every fifteen minutes. They have no sense. Little sense of direction. No jockeys. No form. You may as well build a bonfire and burn the lot. The dogs. Your money. None of this could be conveyed to Jack. He enjoyed the spectacle. Being part of the scene. When he died – he left no money.

When my parents asked for one of my father's sisters – the youngest – to travel to England to help my mother when she was having me – my parents got more than they bargained for. They hoped to get a nurse on the cheap. Instead of getting the youngest and prettiest of the family – my aunt Kathleen – when they opened the door to our house the eldest girl – already thirty five years old and unemployed – was standing on the doorstep: my aunt Nellie. Nellie was hilarious but very idle. Unemployment was rife in Ireland. Casual labour was the order of the day – parodied in the job advertisement concocted by one of my relatives: 'Wanted. A boy as big as a man to ride a bike as big as a bus.' Nellie was also full of blarney. She loved reading about as much as she hated hard work or anything that smacked of routine. We were told she would happily read a brown paper bag but never make a meal. The most she ever managed was a salad. A piece of lettuce. A tomato. A bit of ham. That was it.

Nellie loved to be the centre of attention and to keep everyone amused. She too was an old fashioned Catholic. Like so many of them, she was deeply hostile to sexual aberration or anything out of the norm. That said, she didn't go in for short hand where blasphemy was concerned. She went long but with affection...'Jaysus Mary and Hooooly Saint Joseph... And all the holy family.'

She was never on time for anything but would always run the last few steps. She was once a year late for an appointment with my mother even though she only lived a mile away. We loved her because she was warm and funny.

Then there was aunt Chrissie – a very goodhearted person but altogether a different kettle of fish. Chrissie was my mother's sister. She ran the shoe department inside Bentall's, the department store in Kingston. She was immensely proud of her position. After twenty-five years of service, her name was entered on the roll call of honour – gold writing impressed on an oak panel outside the management floor of the shop. She was prim and proper and stiff. I could never imagine anyone having sex with her or her wanting to have sex with anyone.

I remember the smell of Chrissie. Leather. Woollen tights. Fifties musk. Held together by a corset of convention. She used to collect us every Sunday lunchtime and walk us from our house, in Kingston, up to Hampton Court – a long walk for little people. The idea was to exhaust us. My mother was desperate to get rid of us for a few hours so she could be with my father. When we weren't walked by Chrissie they would bank up the fire after a hefty meal so that we would fall asleep – and they could go to bed and make love. A harmless project after a week of grinding work. Being Catholic was hard on them. They were in love – but you weren't meant to make love. Years later I was to discover a packet of Durex in my father's wallet – a guilty secret.

There was another reason for the walks. My relatives had been brought up surrounded by greenery, sandy beaches, and open skies. They loved the green of the landscape and the flowers of Hampton Court's gardens. Those colours are imprinted on my heart. They are the bright colours of my paintings.

My parents chose England over the U.S. because of its proximity. And because my father wanted us to be well – educated and healthy. He was willing to work very hard for these things in Welfare Britain by paying his taxes. While my mother was less certain, my father could see the bigger picture and bought into it.

When my parents had just three children, we were able to live pretty well on my father's wage. We ate very well. My mother would walk to Kingston's fruit, meat and vegetable market most days and bring home fresh produce – cooked on the day. She cooked three meals a day, seven days a week.

To earn a bit of extra money, when the circus came to Kingston, my father helped set it up. We also had holidays, almost invariably to Waterford to visit our relatives. We were able to enjoy some of the fruits of the consumer society. Not a lot, but some. There was great excitement when the tape recorder arrived – a big chunky piece of machinery that we struggled to conquer. We did not get a television until the late 50s and had to make do with watching it in other people's homes. The first images I ever saw were of a cricket match – I was spellbound.

My parents had six children – born in two lots. My sister Valerie, who was to become the anchor of the family, was born in 1948 – a post-war baby boomer. I was born three years later, followed by my brother Paul who was born in 1954. There was then a five year gap until my brother Tom was born, followed by Angela in 1962 and finally my brother John in 1964.

This was a big team to support on a meagre salary. Of course they knew that they had bitten off a great deal but in those days – especially in Catholic families – having six children did not seem too overwhelming. I was told we had relatives in Ireland who had twenty-two children – enough to stage the FA Cup Final.

My sister Valerie tried to hold it all together. She loved my father dearly. He loved her dearly. She knew him better than anyone. In some ways better than my mother. They were very close. In her heart and in her head they will always be so.

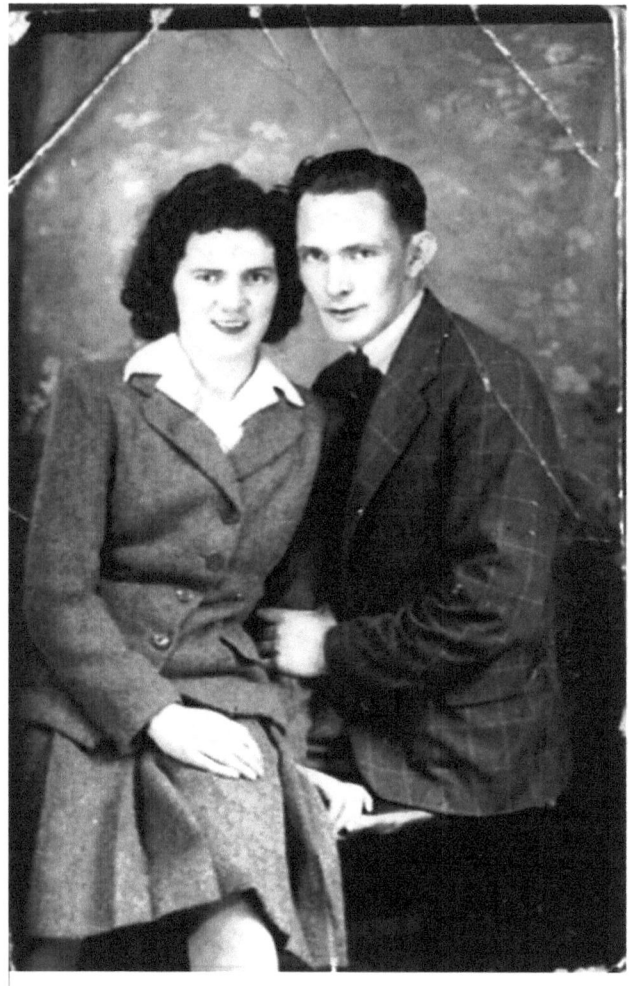

My parents

Valerie appealed to my father's heart and to his intellect. When I was growing up I looked up to her. She knew things. She was strong.

My brother Paul is a very kind and gentle person. Decent. He is very skilled at things for which I have no talent. He is an electrician by trade. A plumber. A carpenter.

My brother Tom has always looked like a Prince. Handsome. Gentle. Incredibly private. You never really know what Tom is thinking. That's the point. He doesn't want you to. Why should he?

Angela is very beautiful. When she was born she arrived in the world with long flowing black locks. She loves my sister Valerie, with all her heart. That is the story of her life. Loyalty. She is also very bright. A successful lawyer. I don't know if she ever lets go.

Then, last but by no means least, my youngest brother John. The stats are frightening. Father dead when he was one. Mother dead when he was eight. He struggled to release himself from the chains of his upbringing. He too is very clever. A successful academic.

As a child, I built a shell around myself. I used to do some weird things. I used to curl my body into a ball and sit inside the tiny wooden box on which the radio sat. Often, they couldn't find me. Once my mother was frantic. Looking back, I think this was an attempt to return to the womb. In the context of my paintings, a bid to remain suspended in the state of empathy for as long as possible and to delay optic.

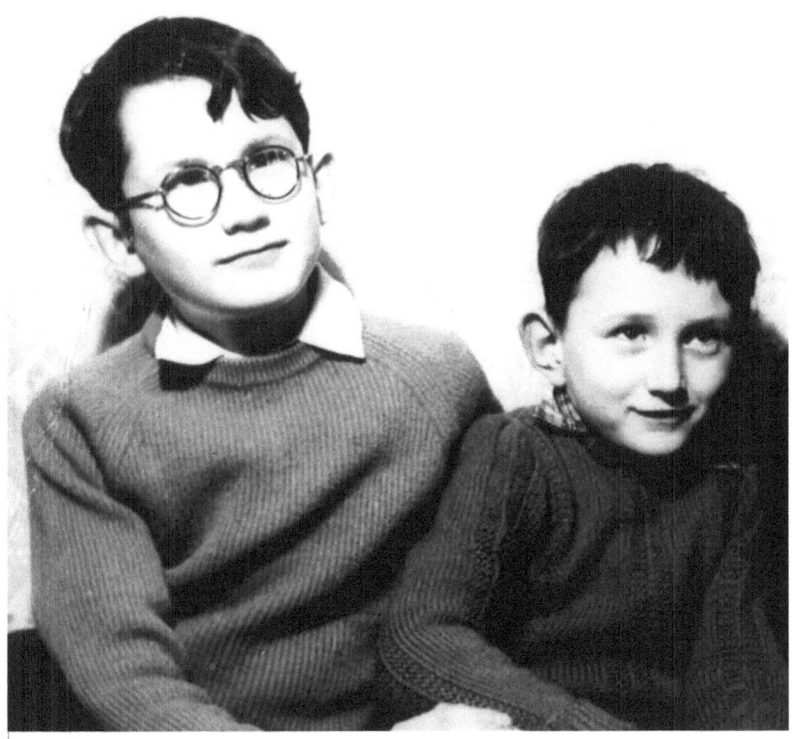

Me & my brother Paul

I was obsessive compulsive. On Friday nights, after school, I would empty the contents of the shed and line them up against the wall of our yard – as if they were for sale. I lived inside my imagination. I used to hide behind the tall dahlias my father grew. I was small enough to be concealed. Hidden by all the colours of the rainbow

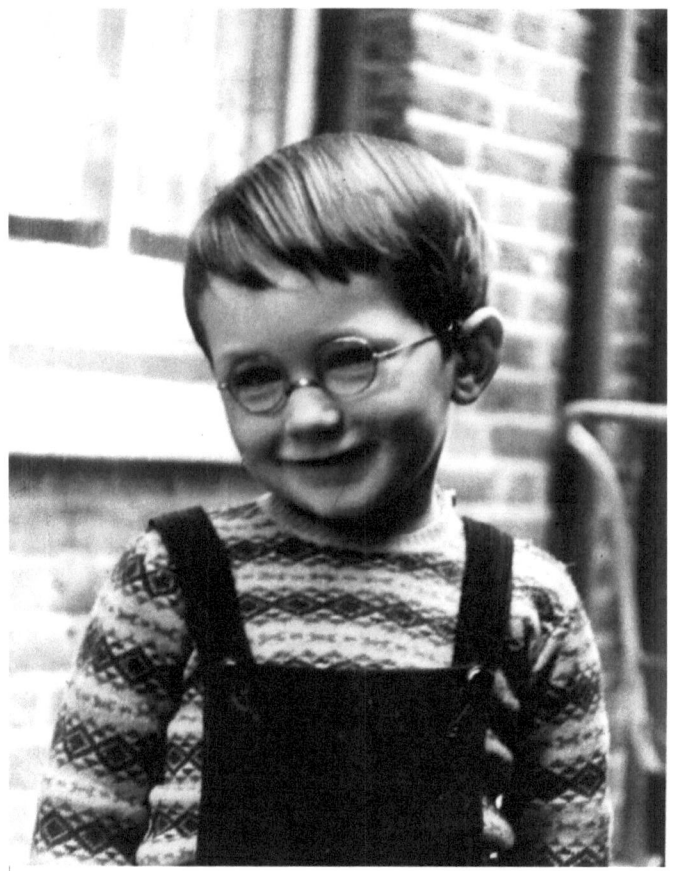

Me, aged 5

and the shiny surfaces of the plants. I also recall the beautiful lilac tree which had to be cut down because it was destroying our garden fence. I remember the day. The sense of loss when it was gone. The absence of something beautiful. I would revisit the colour – purple – in 'Strangers'.

I think I became aware of myself early on because as a family, we were marginal. My father was a brilliant guy but was forced to live the life of an ordinary guy. My mother didn't want to be in England – except for him. She never fitted in because she never wanted to fit in

As the first children of the welfare state in the fifties coming from the background we did, we were huge beneficiaries. For a start we had a G.P who we did not have to pay every time we visited him. He came with the taxes. Likewise, state education. With little money and six children it was a big relief to my parents to know that our health would be taken care of along with our education. My father was a very hard working man –

never out of work. In return we were constantly going to the G.P, to different clinics for injections against the diseases that haunted my parent's generation. We were stuffed full of substances supplied by the NHS. Remember that my parent's generation were terrified of TB and of polio. They determined that we would get neither. I remember being lined up, Valerie, Paul and I, each morning in the winter and being spoon fed with malt and cod liver oil, followed by NHS orange juice and a bowl of steaming porridge.

Despite all the attention, to the despair of my mother, we were as thin as sticks and as white as sheets. One day, despite a healthy breakfast, I was sent home from school by the headmistress, Miss Kenefick, because she thought I looked as though I was going to faint. When I appeared at the front door, my mother was both disappointed and disgusted at the sight of me. She was desperate for a bit of space away from us all, when she could listen to 'Music While You Work' on the radio or read 'Women's Own' – she loved Mary Grant's problem page. Silence was a rare commodity in my mother's life. She had the telephone taken out of the house years later because it kept ringing. I told her that was what it was meant to do.

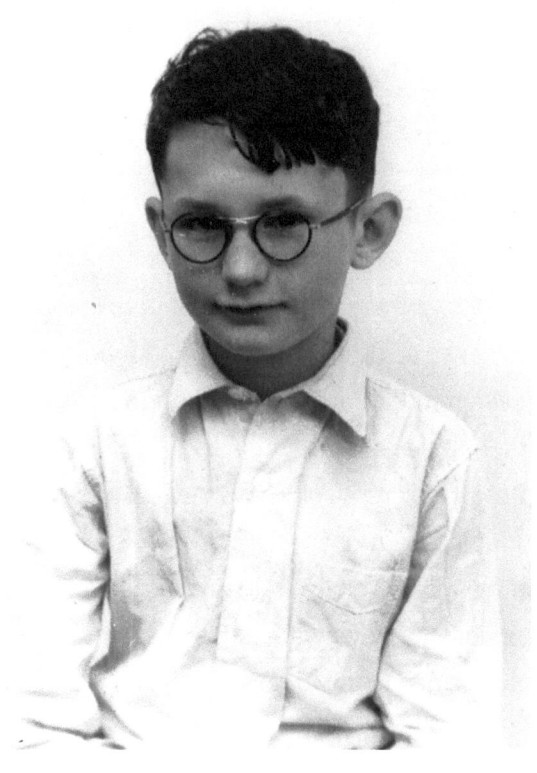

Me, 1959

I was incredibly close to my mother. I absorbed her love for my father. I shared many of the same characteristics. She was very shy. I would cling to her dress. Her dresses, in the style of the fifties, had a lot of fabric around them. She liked the safety of her house and home. She didn't much like society. She knew who she was and was disinclined to give it away. Consequently, I went to school very late. I remember my first day. I sat on the rocking horse and refused to come off. For years, if my mother was passing by the school, I made her kiss me through the railings. She used to have to do a circle to avoid the school.

When we went on holiday to Ireland, I refused to take off my jacket. My clothes were made for me by a seamstress aunt. With my glasses, my navy blue jacket, white shirt and blue bow tie, I looked like a very young Sir Robin Day – the famous broadcaster whose editor I was to become at the BBC years later.

I used to like playing marbles. I loved the glass. The flecks of colour. I liked crunching them against each other. Glass on glass. Ironically, I was very good at playing marbles. Possibly because of a long reach. Possibly because my mono-vision made it easier to throw in a straight line. I never made any friends playing marbles. That was not the point. I liked competition. Winning. Acquiring things. The same went for tea cards. I collected a lot of them. And flags of the world which you could buy for 1d with a bit of pink chewing gum. I would stack the cards up against the wall alongside my house – or up against the school wall. Whoever knocked down the most cards won. On reflection, I think I was drawn to the colours even then. I think the marbles equated to the eye – Optic – and the flags to a celebration of colour that runs through my paintings.

Strangely, at primary school I was the leader of one of the biggest gangs. I came to understand – around the age of ten – that people responded to me. That they would follow. The fact that I was different drew them to me. That's the way it has always been. It is as if they understood that I would go on regardless – with them or without them. That marked me out. I was ambitious.

Later on at secondary school, I would reject the woodwork room, the metal work room – in favour of the Art room.

I knew nothing about Biology – I was never taught it – but I liked the look of the plants standing in glass tubes of water. This was a small bit of something natural, something soft, in what seemed to me to be a horribly hard and unforgiving environment. This was a secondary school for boys whose destiny was to be the factory. I was having none of it. My father had taught me to look up, not down.

When you are as close to your mother as I was, the intrusion of other human beings is difficult. Then there was Dr Scott, our local G.P, who looked like Hitler and behaved like him. He had been an army doctor. These were brutal days. There was no time for the bedside manner of today. When, at the age of nine, I developed terrible asthma Dr Scott was called. My mother said, 'He thinks he's going to die.' To which Dr Scott replied 'Well we all have to die sometime.'

As far as I can tell, we lived in a tight-knit, entirely enclosed world, until I was about seven, in 1958. I certainly did. It was empathetic. Nothing really touched us. Cradle to grave employment. Cradle to grave emotion.

Although I did not want to go, school offered me a source of inspiration. Paint. In the fifties, resources were made over to schools in abundance. A land fit for heroes and all of that. This meant that I could consume school – bought, powder paint of some quality. I was immensely turned on. I don't think I have ever been good at drawing, but I have always been able to paint. Now I had the chance. A method of expression. Something I needed. Something I wanted. Every colour and texture was available to me. At the age of seven, behind my back, I could hear my schoolmates and my art teacher say in hushed tones, 'He's an artist.' It made me feel good. But that's not why I did it. I did it because I had to. As I do today. The colours were luxuriant and free. I wanted to be free.

Paint took me away to another place. I needed my own space. I was fascinated by the rainbow. By texture. By light. It lifted me up and out.

Paint teaches you a lot about yourself. It fights you. It responds. It interacts. I learnt some important lessons simply sitting alone with the paint in the classroom. I loved wet days because I could avoid going out into the playground, and could paint alone. I learnt to take risks. Paint will always challenge you but if you stick with it, it will respond and get you out of trouble. I also learnt not to overdo it. Because I could not afford to buy any paint, I tended to overwork the school paint. Often painting brilliantly at first only to fuck it up out of sheer boredom. Paint also lay behind one of my most abiding beliefs – that beauty is probably the ultimate justification for human existence. Years later, I was to read this in Somerset Maugham's greatest work (although not my favourite) *Of Human Bondage*. My favourite is *The Razor's Edge*.

At home, as a six year old, I exempted myself in order to paint. I painted everything. Lots of sand (echoes of Tramore in Southern Ireland) lots of trees (echoes of Home Park at the foot of Kingston Bridge) and a host of blues. I also painted the Catholic scenes – the stations of the cross – having been given various booklets to colour in.

For some reason, for me, the colour had to be thick and textured. I have always been drawn to impact, to richness – perhaps because we had none. I don't know. But there it is.

So we lived in a bubble. An immigrants' bubble. We empathised with each other – inside a shell. We were inner-oriented and extraordinarily innocent. We were taught to believe in the goodness of mankind. We were optimists.

So, on reflection, I think I started to look outwards. I didn't always like what I saw. And in doing so, I missed the certainty of my mother. But I did it. It was not comfortable. Nor was it easy. It involved rejection of what went before.

Although we lived in our own bubble at home, we were exposed to news of the outside world. My parents were addicted to the radio in the 50s. The day was punctuated by the main news bulletins.

As children we were aware of some big political events. At the age of five, in 1956, I remember the invasion of Hungary and the sympathy my parents and relations had for the people of Hungary – fighters against Communism. Around that time I was admonished by my aunt Chrissie – who could be stern and censorious. As I cut the fat off the meat on my plate and attempted to push it to one side, a heavy hand came down onto mine with the knife in it and pushed the fat back to the centre of the plate, 'Children in Hungary are starving,' she said. 'Send it to them then,' I replied. I was cheeky.

Outside of the house in those early years, I was still very shy. With one eye a lot stronger than the other, I used to hang my head alarmingly to one side. My mother was terrified that I would go blind, and conveyed this thought to me. She also hated dogs, and passed on her deep seated fear to me. When we went out shopping she would veer dramatically from one side of the road to the other to avoid a stray or yapping dog. I became phobic about dogs as a result.

My shyness went hand in hand with a highly-strung and nervous disposition as a child. This was made manifest in very bad asthma which afflicted me into my early teens, only to disappear once inhalers were invented. They were the prop I needed. The asthma was not helped by the fact that our house was very damp and dust collected with great ease. Despite the purchase of one of the new Goblin vacuum cleaners, great wraiths of dust, like rolls of wool, lay beneath each of the beds.

The beds didn't help either. With a family of six children living in a three bedroom house – the situation in 1964 – we were obliged to share a bed between two. I hated it.

I used to put a pillow between myself and my brother. Only when my father died, was I gifted the small box room. Some conciliation.

I was expected to take on certain responsibilities at a very young age – albeit still inside the bubble. Some of the tasks were very nice. My parents loved meat. I was taught how to choose a joint of beef: thickness, marbling, freshness. And was dispatched at a very early age down the end of the road to Whitney's, the local butcher. There I was to pay no more than 8 shillings and 9 pence on the family joint for cooking on Sundays. Like most people of that generation, we then ate the left-overs cold on Mondays. It was my job to ensure that the joint would stretch. It had to be big enough. My parents wanted me to choose alone. To take responsibility. To acquire a skill. I remember the very first day I walked to the butcher's – just two hundred yards from home. The smell of blood. The sight of it. In those days whole carcasses were hung from big hooks with the blood left to drip down onto the sawdust floor beneath. I nearly vomited. The joints of beef were slabs of bloody flesh. When I pointed to one, the butcher slapped it onto the scales and wrapped it in coarse white paper – the same off-white wrapping as the host. I instinctively connected it with the death of Christ upon the cross. As devout Catholics we never ate meat on a Friday or consumed blood. In my paintings, a lot of what I felt that day is replicated. The reverence. The deconstruction. The different interpretations of Christ.

My father also encouraged me to be his adviser. So, at the age of ten, we travelled together to the new town of Havant where my father could have relocated with Avery Hardle, if he had chosen. We looked around a brand new house. At the end of the tour, he turned to me and asked, 'Shall we buy it?' I did not want to move from Kingston – children are very conservative. So I replied, 'You shouldn't be asking me that question. How should I know, I am only ten!' Nonetheless, he pressed on and we looked at various houses, including Lingfield Avenue in Kingston, before he eventually chose to move to New Malden when I was eleven and about to go to secondary school.

Another instance was the Nuremberg trials – or rather the film of them. My father took me to see it one Saturday evening. It was made in black and white and had a terrible impact on me. But that is what my father wanted. He was a Bevanite socialist. I used to eat my dinner opposite the small bookshelf which contained his collection. Amongst the books was Aneurin Bevan's *In Place of Fear* – a testament to the Welfare State. My father wanted his son to appreciate the evil of fascism. He was no fan of communism either. Catholicism saw to that.

Sex is the continual pre-occupation of the Catholic. Despite having six children, my mother was squeamish about sex. She never discussed it. We had no sex education whatsoever. We had to find out about it for ourselves.

Sex helps you to break out of the bubble – or it did in my case. Having discovered masturbation, I found myself ducking and diving around authority – in the form of the Catholic church. In order to escape committing a mortal sin or of being in such a state, we went to confession a lot. Ushered into a small dark room, with a priest the other side of the grill, we would be expected to confess all of our wrong doings. Which I did. 'Father forgive me for these are my sins since my last confession...I stole something...I hit somebody...I was cruel. I didn't mean to. Honest.' 'Three hail Marys and three 'our Fathers' should do it...Give my regards to your mother.' That was the trouble. There was no anonymity. The priest knew the family. He knew my mother. He knew my voice. So when it came to confession, I danced around the issue of sex. Despite the evident interest from the other side of the grill, I refused to be trapped. 'I have had unclean thoughts father.' 'What unclean thoughts?' 'Just unclean thoughts.' No mention of masturbation or as the church would have it, self-abuse. Not on your nelly. Behind the obfuscation lay something more serious. A growing away from the church. A growing away from obedience and conformity. The gradual emergence of an independent spirit. Independent thought. The same thing applied at home. Sex was off limits. So private thoughts spread. Something was withheld.

Years later, I got the nearest to sex education I was ever given when a bunch of Jesuits visited my secondary school to indoctrinate us in the Catholic creed. Under pressure they tried to explain to us the 'birds and bees.' A very fat Jesuit, who looked like Friar Tuck – clearly embarrassed – drew a picture of a pin man and woman on the board. Not a bump in sight. He circled the hands of the male and exclaimed, 'Keep your hands on the desks boys and everything will be alright.' And proceeded to clean the board.

My mother seemed to be always having babies or to be recovering from having them. In the fifties and early sixties women spent a week or two in hospital if they were having a child. Childbirth took its toll on my mother. She often said that when she had me all her hair fell out – and her teeth. She was also plagued with varicose veins – due no doubt to standing up all day washing, cooking and cleaning. Life was hard. There were not many mod cons. Just the daily shopping routine was arduous enough. Vegetables had to be scrubbed and peeled. The volume of washing up was huge. It used to take up to two hours to wash up after Sunday lunch. It was inevitably followed by tea for some of my aunts and uncles. And more washing up. I found the whole routine exhausting.

As the fifties drew to a close our collective eye was increasingly drawn to the outside world, which was in a way just as well, given what would happen to us in the next decade. We were excited by the space race and moved immensely by the election of John Kennedy as US President. He was our man. Young. Handsome. A breath of fresh air. And of course, both a Democrat and a Catholic. Norman Mailer wrote that if John Kennedy was elected US President, it would be an existential moment in US history. He was right. My parents followed the election very closely, especially my father. By then we had our television and were able to watch the television News.

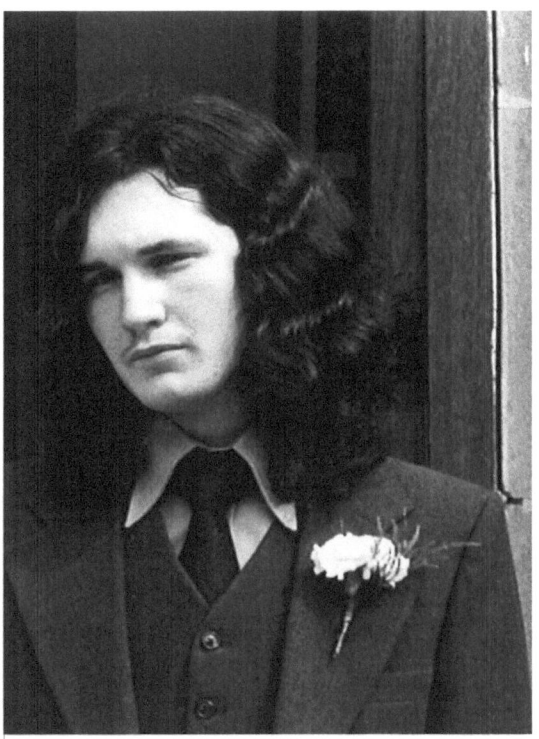

Me, aged 20

My parents liked the family man image, albeit that this turned out to be manufactured. There was very little cynicism in our young family at this stage. We consumed the PR image: Young, virile, family man. Children playing in the Oval office. Beautiful loyal wife. Gets the vote of the people. Our type of people. The liberal left. The significance of Kennedy in our house was that people like us – Irish Catholics – could succeed and get to the top. When I went to University, I was to read Theodore White's 'The Making of the President,' which unmasked the whole event. But for now we lapped it up.

The arrival of the TV in our house was a very potent thing. Not only was it new and exciting, it linked us to the outer world. We began to see things differently. We started to appreciate different countries and cultures. Geography was always taught in a very boring way in the schools we attended. But TV brought the globe alive. It also brought sport into the house. I loved horse racing – as did my father. And football. We watched together as my father's team – Spurs – won the FA Cup Final. Even so, I frequently preferred my own company. After dinner I would stay on in the living room to paint. As the heat dissipated from the room, it became quite cold. My parents could not afford to keep the fire going in more than one room at a time. So I sat alone – enjoying my own company – a bit cold but enjoying the space to paint.

As a child – and even more as an adolescent – I was aware that my left eye sees a bit like a broken digital picture in which some of the '0's and '1's are missing. I felt better about it all one day when an optician told me 'You shouldn't worry so much. You have vision. You can see things other people cannot.' I was willing to believe him. Certainly my left eye has given me a ready-made ability to abstract even the most complex of images and, more importantly, to abstract concepts. So I recall three images from my childhood paintings (up to the age of thirteen) which I have recreated as an adult: the oval shape which reflects light, the prism that reflects the rainbow. The single rock lying on a flat surface – probably the moon.

My father always encouraged me to be my own person – to have ambition. He spotted my love of horse racing and saw that it could be used to great effect. I learnt to read by reading the racing pages. And he could see the potential in my paintings. He used to look over my shoulder whilst I was painting. He frequently told me that he loved the use of colour. It meant a lot to me.

At Christmas – always a huge event in our household – my parents bought me water colours and little pots of enamel for painting models and historical figures.

By the time that my sister Angela was born in 1962, money had become very tight. To cope, my father worked longer and longer hours, as did my mother at home. Although things were tough financially, they were making progress. They planned to sell the house in Kingston, for which they paid £1,000 in 1951, for £3,000 – which they eventually did in 1963. My father could see the prospect of a better standard of living, so long as he could get us to the point where we could begin to look after ourselves.

My mother was getting more and more tired of the daily grind. She used to long for the day when we were all grown up. She yearned for more time with my father. A bit of fun. The nearest she got was holidays in Ireland to visit our relatives and a week in Clacton, when my father used some of the proceeds from the sale of the house to take us away on holiday there. I remember my father coming home with the sale proceeds – paid in cash – and excitedly emptying the bundles onto the kitchen table.

Events started to infringe on our lives – pricking the bubble on a fairly regular basis. The Cuban Missile crisis was a terrifying episode for us as a family – as it was for families throughout the world. There was a struggle to come to terms with the permanent reality of nuclear weapons and the ever present fear of nuclear war. My parents were realists. They knew that you could not disinvent nuclear weapons. My father's hero, Aneurin Bevan, had famously denounced the unilateralists in the Labour party, begging them not to send him 'naked' into the conference chamber.

We experienced the Cuban Missile crisis at home as if all our Good Fridays had come rolled up into one terrible long day of deepest gloom and darkness. It was as if God had turned his back on us, or we had turned our backs on God. Looking back, Cuba was a pre-echo of 9/11. In my mind's eye, I think we feared that the imagery in the 'Blood' series of my paintings would erupt there and then. There was a deep sense of horror of what might have been. As well as a sense that one day such a thing would come to pass.

When the Cuban Missile crisis was finally over, no one was quite the same again. Even so, Cuba was for us still more or less inside the bubble. And not even the assassination of John Kennedy in November 1963 – which was an earth shattering experience – pricked the bubble entirely. We felt Kennedy's death very deeply. We followed every step of the story with ghastly fascination, deep sadness, and huge regret. We knew all the names – Lee Harvey Oswald, Jack Ruby, Lee Radswell and, of course, all the Kennedys. There was a real sense of loss.

In 1964 events started to accelerate and the fabric of our lives started to unravel. By then we had moved from Kingston to a 1930s property in New Malden by a railway line. It was a better house but I never liked it. I left it at the earliest opportunity. I always found it spooky. I don't know why.

I went to secondary school in September 1963 – an all boys Roman Catholic School. My parents had moved so that I could walk to school – about two miles – and my sister could walk to Holy Cross convent. We were still settling into school and our new home when my father started to be ill.

At first none of us thought very much about his illness. After all he was our hero. He began to get terrible headaches. Then terrible sweats. He started to lie on the sofa – or settee as we called it – unable to move or do anything. He was in increasing pain. The GPs, Doctors Boxall and Delauny, were defeated. They had no idea what was wrong with the poor man. At one stage they basically told him to pull himself together. Then they told him he was suffering from a case of food poisoning. He wasn't. He was in severe pain. For months the only medication he received was Anadin purchased from the local newsagent, washed down with lemonade. He developed an unnatural thirst. Eventually, in the summer of 1965, he was admitted to St Mary's hospital in Paddington. There he underwent rigorous tests which almost certainly weakened his heart. He was also a very heavy smoker, which could not have helped. His fingers were black – a deep hue – from the nicotine. He began smoking as a very young child – before the age of ten. Still unable to detect the cause of his illness – and his increasing pain – the doctors decided to open him up on the operating table. There, at the age of forty-five, he died. His heart gave out. The bubble burst like a tidal wave. At the post mortem it was pronounced that he died of a fairly rare form of cancer behind the kidney, a condition called pheochromocytoma.

I was the last person – along with my younger brother Tom – to see my father alive. We had travelled to London to visit him. He got up from his bed in St Mary's to walk us back to the station. He took us to Waterloo. He wore a grey suit, white shirt, black tie. He was always very smart away from work. As we waved goodbye to him, leaning out of the window of the train, I had a sick feeling. I don't know what it was. I certainly did not expect him to die. None of us did.

My mother was distraught. When the hospital called, they called through to our next door neighbour, Mrs Phillips. A kindly busy body. We had no phone. The person at the end of the line asked my mother if she was alone, or if she had anyone to support her. There was no one, just us. My sister, Valerie, who was just seventeen years old, was away on holiday in Clacton at the time. When my mother was told that my father was dead she let out a haunting, deeply anguished cry. She wept. She looked like death herself. And she began to rock. In the months that followed she was inconsolable. She would sit in the corner of our sparsely furnished living room, staring into the middle distance. Disbelieving what had happened. Uncomprehending. Just rocking, rocking, rocking.

My aunt Nellie came to the house quite quickly after the news. We as children, I was only thirteen, were kept in the dark – as an act of kindness. They decided that we should have a night's sleep before being told. What we were told was that Daddy was in trouble. That the operation had not gone well. We went up to bed fearing the worst but full of hope that God would help our father pull through. We knelt and we prayed. Being the eldest child present – I lead the prayers. Unusually for me I awoke early. I remember the light. It was hard and unforgiving. I went downstairs. The atmosphere was appalling. My aunt Nellie sat in front of me. She told me my father had died. It was the biggest shock of my life. I remember the sensation I felt as if it were yesterday. I felt as though a huge and heavy stone was flung at speed from inside the top of my skull down to my boots. The sensation akin to the fast drop of a lift plunging from the top to the bottom floor.

I could not believe that my father was dead. It was so sudden and unheralded. He was so vital. My mother never got her head around the idea that a loving God could allow such a thing to happen. 'We needed him so much. I needed him.' But he was gone. My mother's faith never fully recovered – a fact that she kept to herself and about which she always felt guilty, until she herself had extreme unction on her death bed. She never forgave God, or herself for feeling the way she did. In my paintings, my mother's response is reflected in the 'Hell' painting done at the time of the earthquake in Haiti – a natural disaster that shook faith.

I needed to be sure that he was really dead. So, like doubting Thomas in the bible, I insisted on visiting the undertakers where my father was laid out. I should not have done so. I walked to the funeral parlour. When I got to the room in which my father lay, I caught sight of his very distinctive forehead and wretched. I remember the colour of his skin, which seemed to be a mixture of milk white and watery urine. I stood at the doorway, unable and unwilling to step further in. I could not do it. Seeing my father there like that seemed to me a violation of how I remembered him in life and how I wanted to remember him in death. I went home with a heavy heart and helped someone – I forget whom – to chose the picture that we would use in the Mass card for his funeral. It was taken from a happy day – the day of Nellie's wedding – in 1958. My father looked good in it: handsome. If he had to choose, he would have chosen that picture. Or so I thought.

In the days that followed, I kept a lot of my emotion bottled up for the sake of my poor mother and for my younger brothers and sisters. I let myself go when Valerie got back home. I remember seeing her coming up the back passage leading to the rear entrance to our house. When I saw her, I ran. She put her arms around me and I cried – a lot. As a child, Valerie was always kind and caring towards me. When I first went to school she would sit in the classroom with me waiting for the other children to arrive. She knew I was shy and apprehensive. Seeing her unleashed a flood of emotions in me. It was hard. A harsh day. The rush of emotion I felt when she embraced me is in the light and warm lines of my dialectic paintings, offsetting the darker lines and dark spaces which also evoke the darkness that descended then.

My father's death was the end of the beginning but it felt like the beginning of the end. It signalled the end of all certainty in one way and the arrival of certainty of a different kind. We had absolutely no money and very little prospect of getting any. We had lost our leader. The architect of the project. All that was left were memories and a broken model. That is not quite true; he left behind a lot of love. Conviction that one day we would begin again – and be happy. Thrive. But for now there was the terrible sense of absence that we all somehow knew that we would carry through life.

My mother needed me to be her psychiatrist. Her therapist. Her emotional prop. For several years she would drag herself through life. The only thing keeping her going was us. My mother always confided in me. Drew strength from my strength. After all she put it there in the first place. So she had the right. There were many very dark days where she could not see through to the other side. I would spend hours with her giving her pep talks. 'We will survive. You will feel better one day. You have a lot to live for. We all love you very much. You must never give in. Do it for Daddy.' When I look into my 'Dialectic' paintings, my eye is drawn down many very dark alleyways: black on black on black in some of them. These were the places and the spaces into which my mother descended, struggling to breathe.

No one wanted me to stay on at school. That much was clear – crystal. When I went into the Sixth From – to ram the point home – the science master – all testosterone and beef – devised a board for school dinners. The idea was that anyone who was staying for school lunch would flip a black square with their number on it. Anyone wanting to bring in their lunch – or buy it in – would leave their black square alone – unaltered – not flipped. 'I believe one boy takes free dinners, would he stand up?' It was me. I refused to either stand up or eat someone else's dinner.

Everyone expected me to leave school at sixteen to help the situation – or simply because that is what poor people do. My elder sister was forced to leave school, at the age of seventeen, immediately after my father's death. She was bright and went to work as a secretary in the Bank of England. Her heart, however, was always in the academic world and, when she could, she took two degrees and began to work as an educationalist.

I only remained at school after my father's death because I was just thirteen. The more I came under pressure to leave school as I approached my sixteenth birthday, the more I dug my heels in. At the age of sixteen, with eight good 'O' Levels under my belt, they refused to teach me at first when I went into the sixth form. 'You won't be able to stay the course,' a lot of them said, alluding to the fact that they knew we had no money. Their opposition to me at this time faded because they came to understand that I was serious about staying on. By now I had decided that I would go to university. Another incident which sticks in my mind: My English teacher, a devout Catholic, a Ceylonese gentleman, dropped his opposition to me taking my place on his 'A' Level course when, in a bad moment, I said to him 'I feel as though God is deserting me.' I never lost my ambition. Nor did I lose my ability to follow the light. In my paintings, even in those most reflective of this period, bright light and bright colours vie with the black, dark shades, hellfire. At the age of sixteen I stopped practising Catholicism because of its sexual politics. By then my belief in God was a universal belief not tied to any one religion. The Christ in my paintings should be read in this way – symbolically, over-arching.

I took three 'A' Levels; English Literature, British Economic History, and British Constitution. I got the best 'A' Level results in the whole school.

I was very thin. When I went to university, at the age of 18, I was 6ft 1" tall and I weighed 9st and 10lbs. A skeleton. You could have slid me into an envelope and paid the normal postage.

I had told my mother at some stage, I forget exactly when, that I would give her my teenage years but then I would leave home. In saying this I knew I was inflicting more pain on her, a second bereavement, but I had to do it for the sake of my sanity and for my talent. It was a terrific wrench when, in September 1970, I packed my suitcase and travelled to Victoria station to catch the coach up to Lancaster, and the campus at Bailrigg. Distraught, my mother went to Ireland because she couldn't bear the thought of me leaving home. At first, I was very homesick, even though I was sick of home. I did not like Lancaster at first, but I gradually came to love it. It was very good to me. I often retrace my steps around the building and think of the people who taught me there. It was a modern campus built in the early sixties. I believe the straight lines of its architecture melded with my reading about dialecticism to create the lines of that series of paintings.

When I was an undergraduate, I became very interested in counter cultural politics. I was interested in non-conformity. I wrote a thesis called 'Close to the Edge' which examined the nature of the May Movement in France which exploded onto the streets of Paris in 1968. These were heady days. The sexual revolution was unfolding. The student movement was gathering momentum and opposition to the Vietnam war was intensifying. My interest in the May Movement led to my interest in the Beat Generation and the Hippie Movement. All three figure very prominently in the second chapter of my paintings and the narrative of Book (2).

The May Movement mixed history and art, and was deeply influenced by Dada and surrealist philosophy. It began innocently enough-in November 1967 when students at the university of Nanterre started to revolt in protest against the ban on male and female students visiting each other in their rooms and staying the night. This rolled into student militancy against authority-against the government and the university authorities. There followed violent demonstrations and the occupation of buildings-barricades and fighting in the streets. For a time the students and the workers of France (but not the communist party) combined forces. Factories were taken over as a wave of strikes spread across the country. Joint student-workers demonstrations were staged.

It burnt out very quickly. By the 30th of June it was over. Yet it made a lasting impression on the psyche of the French nation, indeed on the counter-culture that swept the world in the sixties.

When I reflect I think I was interested in this phenomenon because in a sense, I too had to start again. I had to invent or discover the art in my life. I had to develop my own symbolism. For a long time it resided in my writing – in my sub-conscious. Then it came out in my painting.

At the end of my second year at university my mother died, at the age of 49. I had known that she was ill for a long time. She had breast cancer. She had had her ovaries removed. But the cancer spread. She had been terrified of cancer. And wouldn't have the word uttered in her presence – like a lot of people of her generation. Cancer was a death sentence. When I came home, in June 1972, she had emptied the house of children in order to speak to me. She never fully admitted to herself that she was going to die. She struggled to find the words. Eventually she gave up and changed the subject. After that she went downhill very quickly.

My sister, Valerie, got married shortly before my mother's death and moved into a house in Teddington. At the wedding my mother was physically sick.

I remember the day my mother died with awful clarity. I knew her death was coming. It didn't take a genius. For the two weeks prior, she could not eat and could hardly drink. My sister's husband visited our house to help. And peeled grapes for my mother. An unaccustomed luxury. Then she started to fade. She could not walk unaided. And was helped to her bed. It was very hot. The house had a spooky atmosphere. With my mother upstairs drifting in and out of sleep, I decided to send my younger brother and sister to Ireland. I had to concentrate on my mother. I played Joni Mitchell records – her mood matched mine 'Blue.' My imagination started to work over time. The day before she died, the air dead still in my bedroom next to hers, I fancied a freak breeze caused the lampshade in my tiny box room to swing backwards and forth. I don't know whether I imagined it or not. I think it happened but I cannot be sure. My nerves were jangling. I think I experienced the meaning of the word void, or rather its existential state. Although in my paintings void refers to the historical reference to the post-war period, I remember to this day the absence of oxygen in the house as my mother lay dying.

On the day my mother died, 18th August 1972, seven years after the death of my father, just eight days in between, he died August 10th 1965, I called the ambulance and requested that my aunt Nellie travel with my mother and I to Kingston Hospital. For all her blarney, Nellie was good for my mother. She could blag it. Lying on the stretcher my mother said to her, 'I am not going to die, am I Nellie?' Nellie replied like the actress she always was, 'Do you think I would be sitting here with you Bridie, if I thought you are going to die?'

When we arrived at the hospital, my mother was taken straight to one of the oldest wards and placed in the bed nearest the exit. The inevitable was beginning to unfold. Once she was settled, for some reason I felt the need to feed my remaining brothers and sisters before returning to the hospital for an evening visit. I bought pork chops. Then I went back up to the hospital taking my nine year old brother, Tom, with me. As we arrived we could see that curtains had been pulled around my mother's bed. A very young and inexperienced nurse came walking towards us. As we stood there, she boldly told us, 'Your mother is dead.' I held Tom's hand and walked to a side room. He said, 'People don't just die like that. She wanted to go skiing.' She never went skiing. The idea of my mother skiing was vaguely ridiculous and out of sync. Yet here was how one of her sons recalled her. Perhaps she had confided this ambition to him in a private moment. Here was a young boy stranded in the middle of nowhere trying to make sense of his mother's death.

When life drains away, it does so quite quickly. Having witnessed my father laid out on the mortuary slate, I could not put myself through it again. I refused to allow a post-mortem to take place on my mother's body – she had been through enough. We all knew what she died from: cancer, the same thing that killed my father. So I left the hospital with Tom. I went to tell my aunt Chrissie who lived in Raynes Park, accompanied by my brother – in-law, Chris. On the way, on the bus, I broke down and started to cry like a baby.

When I got home I really let myself go. I wept the way my mother wept when my father died. I had bottled up so much for so long. I was distraught. Without my father, without my mother. I felt more alone than ever before. Utterly. But in truth I felt free.

My mother was buried on a blazing hot day – in Kingston cemetery, alongside my father. Grave E17.

My father's sister, Anastasia, loved my father a great deal. So much that she carried a big bag of painted stones – all the way from Staines to Kingston cemetery. Where she placed them on my parents' grave.

After my mother's death there was a hiatus while we considered what to do. My elder sister was twenty-three years old. I was twenty. Paul seventeen. Tom thirteen. Angela ten. John eight. My sister was married with a child on the way. Her husband, Chris, a good man, had been to the London Business School and had prospects. We considered splitting the family up. I knew I could not support a family on a student grant.

After a little while, a few days, Val and Chris decided to keep the family together. They moved into the house in New Malden and set about turning it into their family home. Drained of energy, I went back to university looking as though I had been run over by a bus.

When I went back to Lancaster in the autumn of 1972, I threw myself into my work. Determined not to be pushed back, I propelled myself forward. Drive comes from a sense of absence. I became a very driven man. I was determined to keep moving forward. I never gave up or felt like giving up. Ironically my faith in God strengthened. My thirst for ideas grew.

I was offered a place to do postgraduate research at St Edmund Hall – Teddy Hall – at Oxford. But first I had to be interviewed at All Souls – the finest and most elite of the Oxford colleges. All Souls had no students. I put off the interview two or three times because I was doing my finals. In the event, I arrived in Oxford the day after I had finished. Exhausted. I was interviewed by four of the world's top academics, chaired by Max Beloff, who held the Gladstone Chair of Public Administration in Oxford and who was a fellow of All Souls. They used a frightening technique. When I entered the room, only Beloff was there. For what seemed like an eternity he grilled me about my research project – a study of post-industrial society and youth culture built around a scholarly history of the beat generation and the hippie movement. This plan was a revolution for Oxford. I had taken a big risk. He was intrigued. He was a man for detail and of great erudition. When he finished interrogating me, a knock came on the door. Enter Pinto Deuschinsky, 'Mr Hogan tell us about your proposal.' The sequence was repeated again – a third, a fourth time. Two exchanges stick in my mind. Towards the very end, my patience wearing thin, Max asked where Aristotle fitted in. 'I am not interested in Aristotle' I replied – arrogantly. Then came the killer question: 'What if we give you a place but no money?' 'Oh,' I replied immediately, 'if you can't afford me, I can't come.' Offended, Beloff said 'Of course we can afford you.' By the time I arrived back in Lancaster an offer had been dispatched to my pigeon-hole by special delivery. I was in.

I loved Oxford. The more I got into it, the more I loved it. I was lucky. I worked under a genius, Bryan Wilson. He had been made a fellow of All Souls, having done his doctorate at the London School of Economics. He was a hard task master. He had created a whole school of academic study – the study of sectarianism and religious sects. He was fascinated by collective behaviour – as was I. He provided me with endless reading lists and directed me to different models to help me understand why the beat generation emerged in the 1950s and the hippies in the 60s. He was also a stickler for

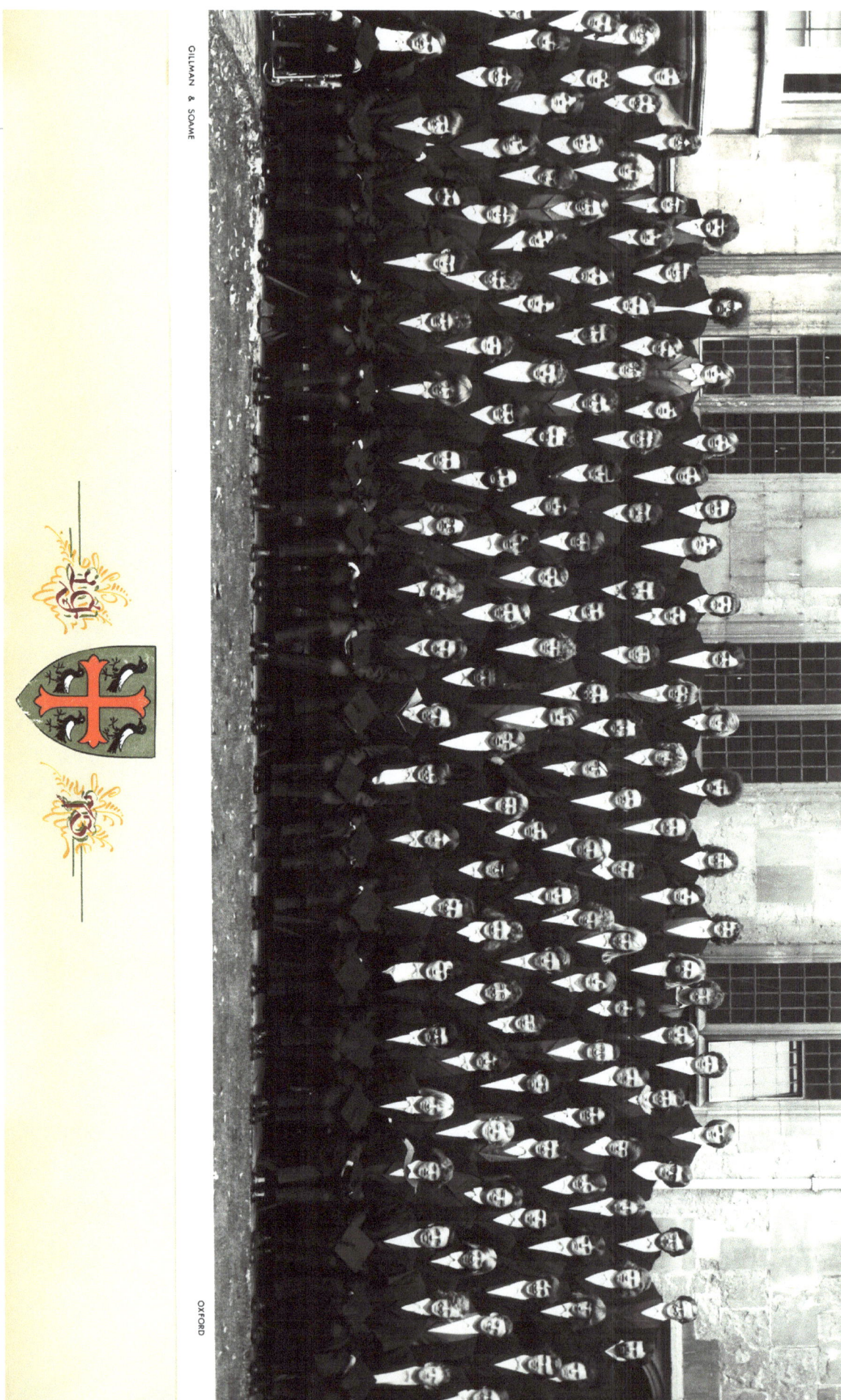

St Edmund Hall, Oxford. Me seated front row seventh from the right

GILLMAN & SOAME

OXFORD

Oxford etiquette. At my first meeting with him in his palatial rooms, rooms where the Pope would not have been out of place, he wanted to get a few things straight. I was to call him Mr Wilson, not Bryan. He would call me Mr Hogan. A bit like surgeons.

In those days, 1973, there were still all-male colleges. All Souls was one of them. However, with some sadness, he informed me that there are some ladies nights these days. But added, in all seriousness and with a straight face, 'I go out on those occasions.' The University as a whole was still predominantly male. Whereas Lancaster was mixed. Teddy Hall was all male. So was All Souls. In a way, I felt like I had gone back to school. My secondary school, Richard Challoner, named after the Catholic bishop, was all boys. Lancaster had clubs for everyone – gay, lesbian, feminist, etc.

My research was a radical departure for Oxford in those days. It would draw together many different strands and influences. It would straddle the conventional and unconventional, culture and counter-culture, political science and social science. It would challenge orthodox opinion. It would get inside the head of the youth culture – not to judge but to understand. It would be very potent. Lots of things, very familiar today but not then, would need to be assessed – sexual politics, racial politics, drug culture, artistic expression, etc.

While I was at Oxford I met my wife, Jane. I fell deeply in love with Jane and we became life-long friends. In lots of ways Jane helped me heal. She embraced me. She was very beautiful. Very clever. Very skilled. She offered me security. I knew she would always stand by me – come what may.

Jane had had a different upbringing to me but a no less potent one. She was the product of a fiery mix. From a genuine, passionate, difficult and troublesome marriage. Her father, Bill, was the uncle of Neil Kinnock, now Lord Kinnock, by 1983 the leader of the Labour Party and the Official Opposition. Bill was the youngest of eight children born into a mining family in Tredegar, South Wales. Aneurin Bevan territory. He was a good but intellectually lazy man. A headmaster, he could not be bothered to test his own prejudices. Instead he luxuriated in the class war, endlessly ranting and raving on high days and holidays, losing his audience in the process. There was no bad in him just a lot of huff and puff. His wife, Eveline, my mother-in-law, was a totally different kettle of fish. She came from an upper middle class family in the boot and shoe industry in Kettering in Northampshire. She fell out with her family when she divorced not once but twice. Such things were frowned upon in those days. She was beautiful. And clever. And she was not frightened of Bill – despite the verbal violence and emotional spasms to which he was prone. They loved each other immensely, although a lot of the time you would have never have known it. They frequently fought like cats and dogs. The reason was quite simple. The egotistical stakes were very high. The clash of classes could be very amusing. Eve, a brilliant cook, (she ran the Lindo wing for private patients at St Mary's in Paddington) would present Bill with a lovely piece of poached salmon and mockingly ask him if he would like HP sauce to go with it.

Jane is the product of Eve's third marriage. Eve had two children by her first marriage – Jane's sister Sally who emigrated to New Zealand in the 60s meeting and marrying Peter Taylor, an outstanding academic specialising in engineering. Sally is one of the most musically talented people I know. Like Bill, her stepfather, who was a great violinist, Sally has a great passion and talent for music. Peter taught the future Vice Chancellor of Oxford University John Hood, who I got to know well and liked. He officiated when my daughter Cassie was awarded her degree at the Sheldonian Theatre.

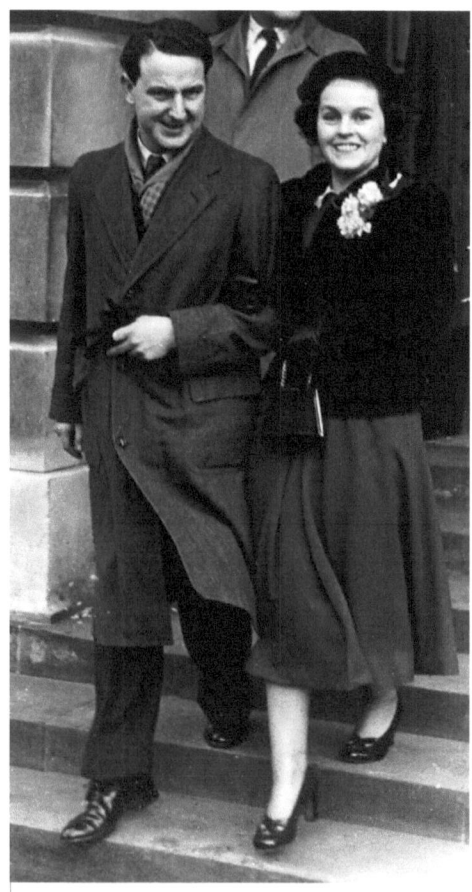

Bill & Eve Kinnock

Bill had a high IQ but a low intellect. He was a truly exceptional bridge player, a decent golfer, a horse rider and did his bit – a big bit – during the Second World War. About which he rarely spoke. For all his foibles he deserved respect. He was a child who never grew up because he did not want to. Eve, who was several years older than him and already tired by the time they married (she was thirty-six years old and had had several miscarriages) was in a lot of ways his mother figure. She would call him 'Billy Boy.' Bill was also brilliant with my son, Alexander, born in 1987. They were two children. They understood each other. They loved to play. Bill was better with men than women. He never really got the measure of them. He found it more difficult to relate to my daughter, Cassie born in 1983. Eve on the other hand loved Cassie and Cassie loved her.

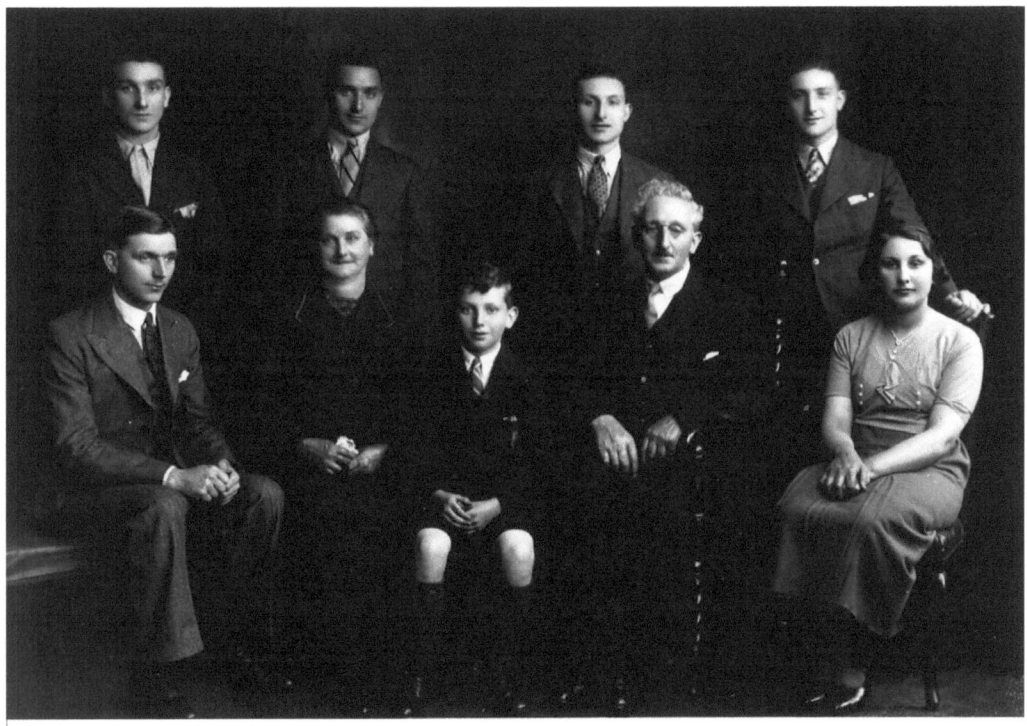

Kinnock family c.1925

Like both her parents and her cousin, Neil, Jane is very charismatic. She is a truly gifted teacher. Fantastic with people of all ages and shapes. By the time I met Jane I was ready for a relationship. I was willing to trust. I also needed to fill the void left by the death of my mother. In terms of my paintings, although the timing is out of sync, Jane was a counterpoint to the void.

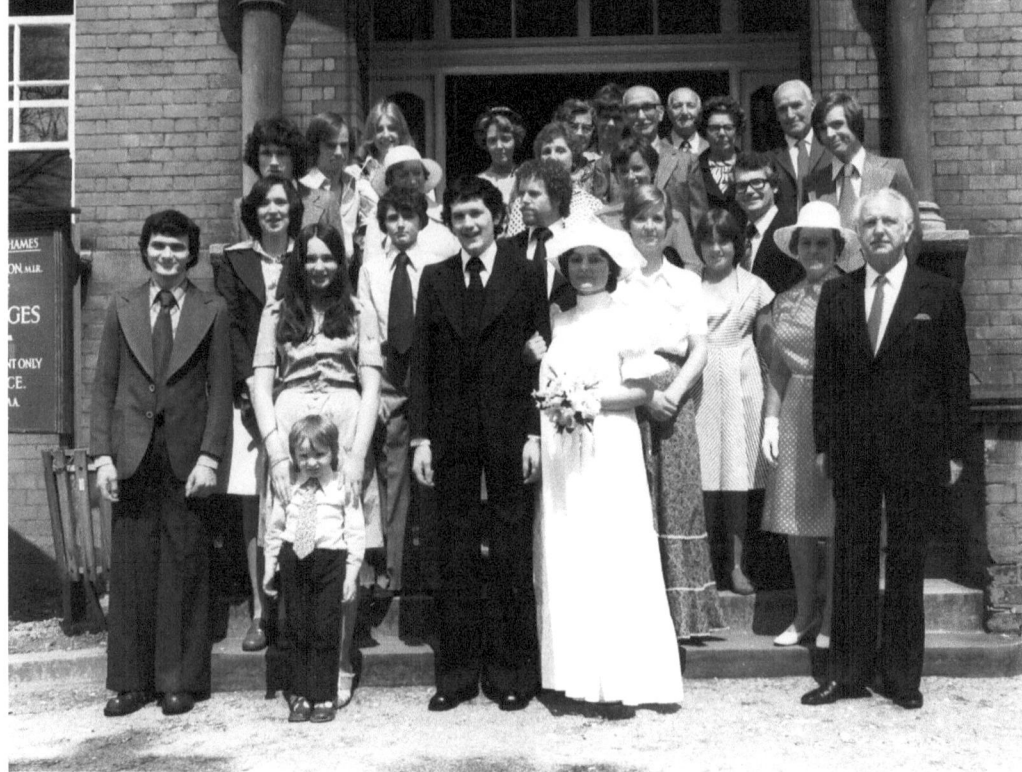

Wedding day

Jane and I moved in together within a couple of weeks of meeting each other in the summer of 1974. We were married two years later on 24thJuly 1976. We found a flat in Stoke Newington that we could afford to rent – £15 a week. We were very short of money. But happy. Jane was working as a newly qualified teacher in Shoreditch in the East End of London, N16. Most of the children were working class, a lot of them deprived, some a touch nuts. The school was brilliantly run by an old-style teacher, a gem called Mrs Shaw. She believed that working class children deserve, indeed require, to be taught the basics – the three 'Rs' – before moving onto anything more complex. These are people who need to be able to hold their own in society and to have jobs. Mrs Shaw believed in this credo. She did a huge amount for the community as a result. She also ran the school, Randal Cremer, with a rod of iron. It was a challenge working in the East End of London in those days. Opposite the school was the house where the notorious East End gangsters, the Kray brothers, were brought up.

Stoke Newington had been a genteel place at the turn of the nineteenth century. By the early 70s it was like downtown New York on a bad day. The only people who lived there were the people who had no other choice. The area was a magnet for immigrants and students. It was riddled with drugs, needles and discarded condoms. Private houses were used as nightclubs – usually run by West Indians. The noise at night could be very loud indeed. Sometimes we would move from the bedroom to the front room to escape it. The police were overwhelmed by the scale of the problem. One morning after the night before, I heard a local Policeman remonstrating with one of the nightclub owners. 'I don't want to speak to you' said the man. 'I am not interested.' The policeman drifted away. The pub a few doors up from our place had strippers most days. I remember taking Jane to a pub lunch there one Sunday – a somewhat middle class idea. There in front of us, standing on a table was a young woman with huge breasts that could fell you at forty paces and nipples the size of apples. No one took any notice. Amazingly. It was also physically dangerous. One night, there was dense fog. I got off the bus near the flat and started walking towards home. Out of the thick mist appeared two young men. Holding a gun. They lifted it to my face and pulled the trigger. Blanks. 'You blinked.' 'Wouldn't you?' I said. And walked on. Afterwards I felt sick. It took me a few minutes to realise what had happened. The danger.

To live in Stoke Newington in those days was to live on the edge. It was a very edgy place. An air of volatility. Risk. You felt it could all go terribly wrong very easily. That there was beneath the surface a battle being waged – the eternal battle between good and evil. During the time we lived there, there were several murders nearby. And women were often beaten up by their boyfriends – or the men who ran them. This knife-edge – writ large – is captured in my paintings in the 'Eclipse' series where good and evil vie for centre stage.

Even then my life was a life of contrasts and extremes. I had moved to London to be with Jane and to use the British Library in Bloomsbury for my Oxford research. In those days the British Library was perhaps the best club in London – certainly for writers. The reading room was regal in powder blue. Magnificent. Like others before me, I would sometimes sit a desk 07 – where Karl Marx sat. It was awe inspiring to feel his presence. I was given access to the beautiful North Library with its huge green leather desks, my own cabinet for storing books and writing materials and to the typing room. Daily I would observe famous writers and academics arrive mid-morning whereon they would do their correspondence, wonder off for a spot of lunch and return to read and write. The gap between the two worlds – Stoke Newington and the British Library – could hardly have been bigger. I associate the powder blue of the central dome with good – echoes of God – in my paintings.

Bloomsbury in the early 70s was a very interesting place – understated – somehow hidden. A place that the natives knew about – the locals – but no one else. Odd. After all, Bloomsbury attracts a lot of tourists. Even so, it retained the air of the 1920s/30s. The Bloomsbury set and all that.

The 70s coincided with the increasingly violent campaign waged by the IRA against the Westminster Government. London was a scary place, with bombs going off on a regular basis. Stoke Newington was, as usual, in the middle of it all. I remember arriving home one night and switching on the news at ten. Bong. Two bomb factories discovered tonight in North London. Bong. 'The first was discovered here – near Amhurst Road, Stoke Newington'. Bong. 'The second discovered up the road also near Amhurst Road.' That road, which runs a lot of the length of Stoke Newington, was where we lived. As soon as I got my job at the BBC we left.

When I graduated from Lancaster and then from Oxford, I was one of a very special breed. Only three or four percent of the country went to university at the time. Anyone with an Oxford degree, let alone a 'Higher' Oxford degree, as I had, was very special indeed. Today, of course, it is the polar opposite. Even so it was hard for me to get my first step up the ladder. So when I applied to be a graduate trainee at the BBC, I knew it was a bit of a long shot. As in the Civil Service, in those days, it was a four-stage process that took the best part of a year.

I had to provide a very detailed written CV explaining why I had applied. The next stage was a face to face interview with four of the great and good of the BBC at the time. Having survived that ordeal, I had to write a script – an obituary for someone famous to be put together in the space of a couple of hours. I chose Henry Kissinger from the list of possibilities. Without having any knowledge of TV – and without having anyone in my family who had ever worked in TV, which marked me out from everyone else on the shortlist – I wrote the script down the right hand side of the page and the visual cues on the left. It just seemed the easiest way to do it. What I did not know was that all TV scripts are laid out in that exact manner. With the help of Jane, whose previous boyfriend had been a cameraman at LWT, I wrote an over the top but memorable testimonial to the life and times of Henry Kissinger along the lines of 'a hundred capitals and a thousand planes.' It took a few minutes to write but it did the trick. The panel loved it. At the final interview, which was in some ways as testing as the All Souls encounter, feeling a bit weary, I finished my grilling by saying to the panel that I did not require any recompense for the bus journey home. I was only living in Stoke Newington at the time. I did not intend to curry favour. However, they liked the gesture. Once again, I was in. And on the way.

In those days, 1978, there were just three television channels, BBC 1 and 2 and ITV. The people running these were judge and jury. They were demigods. And they behaved like demigods. They decided who would get the break and who would not. To be turned down by the BBC was virtually to be excluded from the television industry altogether. Getting in depended on their grace and favour.

I joined the BBC as a graduate trainee in 1978. I was a great success very quickly. Certain events stick in my mind. They taught me things and had an influence on the way I see the world and on my painting.

In the summer of 1981, I was asked to make the life history of a truly remarkable man – the extraordinary ordinary man as Marcia Williams called him – Harold Wilson, the former Labour Prime Minister. I had always admired Wilson. Intellectually gifted, Harold had worked under William Beveridge, the architect of the welfare state at University College in Oxford. By the time he retired, in 1976, he had spent forty years on the front bench.

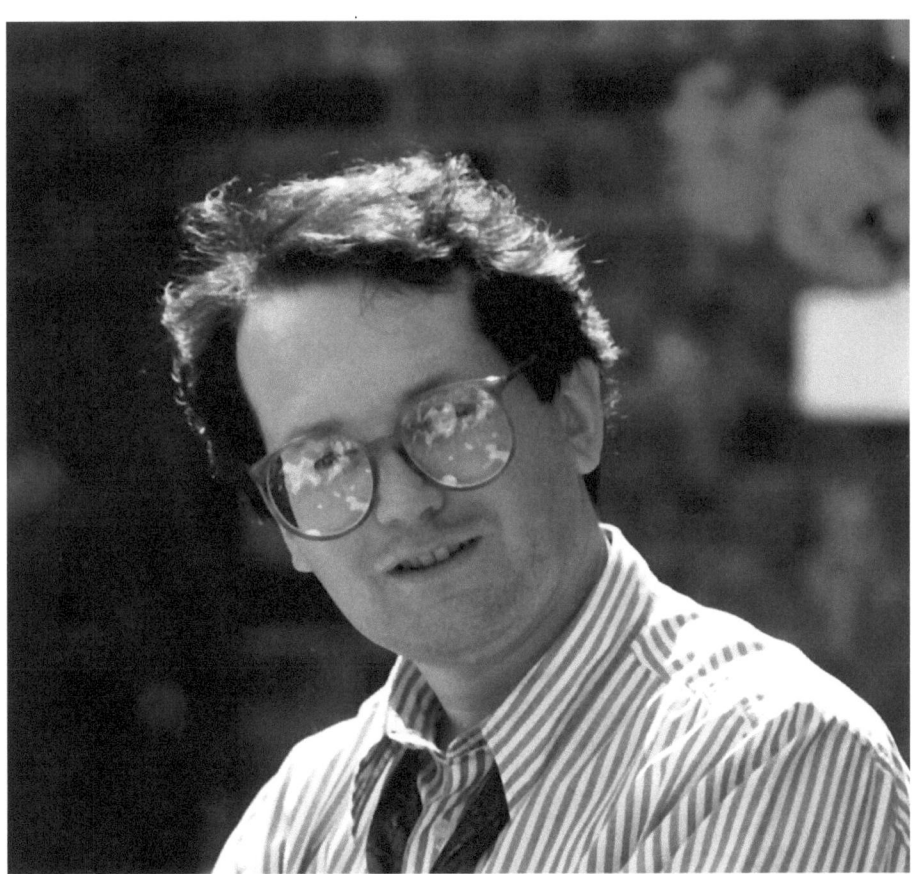

I joined the BBC

I was asked to produce four programmes about his life and times. I could not say no. So I did it. Wilson had won four elections out of five. He was clever. He was shrewd. He played politics like a game of chess. He was also neurotic. I got to know him over a period of intense immersion that probably lasted no more than three or four months. I had been given a gift. The chance to encapsulate his life and times.

It seems ridiculous now but in the sixties, Harold was the nearest thing that we in the UK had to John Kennedy. Albeit that, as far as I could tell, he didn't seem to be interested in extra-marital sex or even in the exercise of power. He was a moderate man. He had been a liberal at Oxford. His sensibilities always lay in this area. He just happened to get involved with the Labour party. That said he could never have been a Tory. Politics is tribal.

When I met him we liked one another. I had done my homework. He liked that. We were to film on the 6th floor of Television Centre – the management floor on which the Director General had his TV offices. This was significant in Wilson's mind.

At the very beginning, I asked him to dwell on what I thought would be the key questions. And to which we would return over the months of filming that would follow. In posing these questions I was aware that Harold's health and mind were failing. Contrary to what has often been said and written, however, he was not mental or dead by the time I got to him. He just wasn't the force he used to be. I knew he had his 'marbles' but fewer of them than he used to have. And he once had a lot.

At the outset, I wanted to get the answer to some very simple and basic questions, 'What are they?' he asked. As usual, suspicious of anyone who worked for the BBC. So what were they? 'Well, what did the white hot heat of technology mean?' – A reference to Harold's speech after he had become the leader of Labour Party and which set the tone for his premiership. What would he like on his grave stone? And why did he resign when he did? 'Alright young man,' he said. 'Don't say now,' I replied. 'Think about it.'

So for many days that summer, in 1981, we would arrive at Television Centre, have coffee followed by lunch and a late tea. Like something out of a le Carré novel, a private eye was always present. Ducking, diving. Looking this way and that. Dirty old raincoat. Not properly shaven. Never eating a proper meal. A dog's life. And, of course, Harold being Harold, there were times when he didn't even want him in the room.

One day, when we got to Harold's resignation he told me to clear the room. There were to be no cameras, no film crew. No detective. He was furious with me.

In my innocence, I had read the Pencourt Files – studied the various theories of why Wilson resigned when he did. I had also spoken to some people in his kitchen Cabinet. I never believed the wild theories about why he resigned.

There was no smoking gun. Harold was not a spy. He was not a communist.

In answer to my questions he answered thus: Question: 'What did the white hot heat of technology mean?' Answer: 'I suppose it meant we weren't going to have any more of that nationalisation clap trap.' Question: 'What would you like on your tombstone?; Answer: '7 out of 10. The country was a bit happier when I left than when I arrived.' A statistician speaks. Question: 'Why did you resign when you did?' Answer: 'Well, I was exhausted. I promised Mary..'

I got the impression that Harold was not interested in the things that drive the majority of people, including most politicians. He didn't appear to have any material or physical weaknesses: As far as I could tell he wasn't interested in money especially, big houses, fast cars, drugs, gambling, or affairs. He was in this sense the perfect politician.

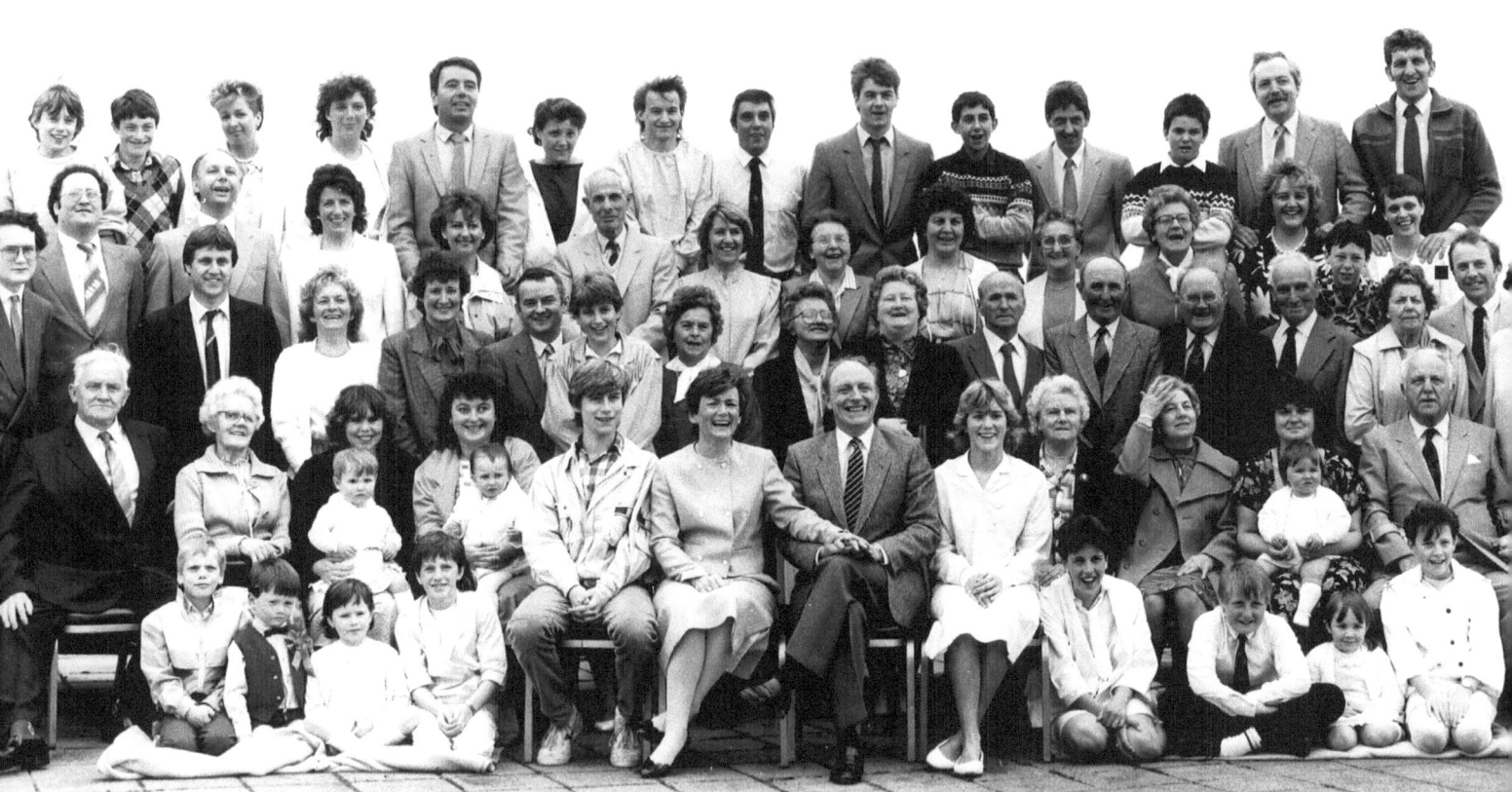

Kinnock family 1984

His work was his life. There did not appear to be any room for anything else. He was one-dimensional. For this reason, at the end of it all, he remained a mystery to me. In fact I concluded there was nothing else. The mystery was the absence of complications. I think he worked so hard because he did not know any other way to be. Then there was his exceptional brain. That drove him on until it gave up on him. Not the other way round. Then he slowed down. And stopped.

At the end of that summer, at the end of all the filming, Harold asked to speak to me privately. Once again there was to be no one else in the room. He wanted to say something personal. I had told him my story. He told me that he was moved. 'Whatever anyone else says to you, be yourself.' I shook his hand and ushered him from the sixth floor of Television Centre to the awaiting car. With that he was gone. We never met again.

From one Labour leader to another . Neil Kinnock had become leader by 1983. Not long afterwards the whole Kinnock family assembled for a get together at The Drury Lane Hotel in London.

The BBC was good for me. It played to my strengths. It gave me a home and a place in society.

I was lucky to work with the people I did at the BBC. Within news and current affairs, I virtually worked with everyone who mattered. Indeed I was their boss. Their editor. I was in charge of Question Time, Elections, Documentaries, a senior producer on Newsnight and Panorama. I was Sir Robin Day's editor, David Dimbleby's, Peter Snow's, Peter Sissons' etc. Along the way I met some very interesting and talented characters – some mad, some bad, but invariably interesting.

The whole of my BBC career was spent based at Lime Grove Studios in Shepherds Bush – the home of the house of horrors, in more ways than one. I hated Lime Grove at first but I came to love it. It was weird. Pipes that looked as though they were dripping with poison. Dark film sets and studios. I once bumped into a dalek late at night – and screamed. 'Make up' where people having affairs would shag. Hospitality rooms laden with booze and food. The club where alcoholics – and there were a lot of them – would hang out. It was a riot. It also was a hotbed of creativity. Some of the best programmes ever made came out of Lime Grove. That said, it always had the air of yesterday – more film set than TV studio.

In those days, Panorama was the high church of documentary making. This was the era when, as they used to say, men were men and budgets were budgets. There was none of today's penny pinching or accountability. No one had the slightest idea what a programme cost nor were they at all interested. The nearest we ever got to budgeting was the occasional edit. Producers would go filming for up to a year using every lens in the box. Occasionally sending back the rushes. They would then reappear. After three or even six months in the cutting room, they would hand over their film. A bit like the way the priest gives out the host.

I remember one bizarre incident. One August – there was literally not a single soul in the office – I got a call at home. Someone very special indeed had contacted the BBC switchboard and had news that would change my life forever. He had to see me urgently. Despite being August it was very dark and gloomy. Always one with a nose for a story, I told my wife I would have to go in. I got into our car and ambled up to Shepherds Bush. I went up to the third floor office. About twenty minutes later, my direct line rang. Whoever it was, was downstairs. The commissionaire would bring him up. In those days commissionaires looked like decorated war heroes. 'Mr Hogan, this is so and so.' In the dark – the lights were off – I was confronted by someone who looked like Jesus Christ. It was no accident. 'Well what can I do for you?' 'I am about to tell you something that will change your life forever.' 'What is that?' 'I am the risen Christ.' 'Don't call us we'll call you,' (or words to that effect), I replied. This sounds like one for Nationwide, I thought.

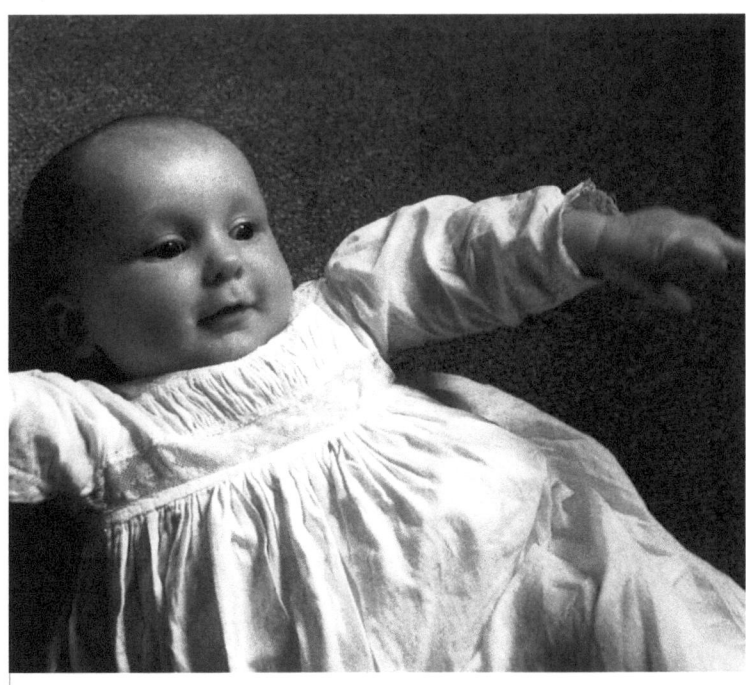

Cassie

The current affairs show was famous for switching from an interview with the Prime Minister to an item about skateboarding ducks. I didn't dare to laugh at the risen Christ because I thought he might attack me.

After the Wilson programmes, I became the producer of the Party Conferences. In those days, prior to the advent of Channel 4, we used to make ninety hours of live television, much of it in peak time, between September and mid – November. No one in their right mind would do that nowadays. People are much more concerned with Strictly Come Dancing and the X-Factor than politics. But back then it was different.

My role was extraordinary. I determined everything. How the set looked. The graphics. The cast list. How long we stayed on a debate. When we cut away etc. No one would be allowed such power nowadays. I used to be supplied with the text of the leader's speeches – a few pages ahead at a time. When Neil Kinnock made the speech of his life – in 1985 in Bournemouth – denouncing the militant tendency in his own party, I was able to put the camera on the chief culprit, Derek Hatton, the leader of the militants in Liverpool, in good time for him to be fingered and for him to repost, 'Liar, liar, liar.'

I joined Panorama in the autumn of 1983. Once installed, I was approached by Phil Pedley, the leader of the young Conservatives, who was deeply concerned about the alleged infiltration of the Conservative Party by a group of racist and anti-Semitic organisations. He had been commissioned by the Tory high command to investigate. He was willing to co-operate with Panorama to expose their activities. Sensing a good story, I was willing to be the conduit. And so the deed was done. The reaction, as I expected, was ferocious. Sensing great danger, the Tory party closed ranks. Witnesses evaporated. Statements were withdrawn. Nightmare.

In the midst of this darkness – bright light. My daughter Cassie was born, five weeks premature, on 12th December 1983. I had it all planned. The day Cassie was born, I had a lunch in Shepherds Bush around the corner from Lime Grove in a nice little Turkish restaurant. The programme was due to go out on the 30th and I expected Cassie to arrive two weeks later. The due date was 21st January – which evidently turned out to be wrong. My friend warned me, 'You cannot plan like that.' 'No. No. All my mother's babies had been born late. It would be fine.' I strolled back to Lime Grove. The phone went. It was my wife. She was very calm. Nothing to worry about but we should just get things checked out. She was feeling a little bit odd. I drove home – no rush – and then went along to the Charing Cross Annex – Shepherds Bush. We had chosen the hospital because it was near to the BBC. It was a very wet and busy night. Babies were literally stacked up in the corridor. We went into the room. The doctor took one look at Jane and announced, 'your baby will be born in the next two hours – max.' Jane immediately changed her tune. She was in labour – rapid labour. Her demeanour changed in that split second. The baby was coming. At five minutes to eleven that night, Cassandra Jane Eveline Hogan was born. She was a beautiful baby with magnificent eyes and fantastic skin. She would grow into a very lovely and talented human being.

Jane was determined to get Cassie home as soon as possible. I was working tremendously hard during the day and at night getting things ready for her arrival. We had bought a house in Durlston Road in Kingston Upon-Thames – a good sized three bedroom Victorian house, but it was still being fitted out. One morning, a couple of days before they came home, I took delivery of a washing machine. Dishwasher. Carpets. It was like a scene from Changing Rooms. Jane eventually came out of hospital on Christmas Eve. I went shopping to find a hamper locally which we could use to get us through the first few days. While I was out, I started to feel unwell. I came down with a nasty bout of flu. I took a few days off. And managed to shrug it off. While I was laid up I made an important decision. I knew the Panorama programme was going to be very controversial. But it had to be done. I would, however, make certain that every line in the chain of command in the BBC was briefed and endorsed the end product. Once the balloon went up, we were all on the same page. Despite our unity as a team, the ferocious attack that followed the programme put me out on a limb. Lots of people hated the fuss. Hated the spotlight. Lots of people needed to be reassured behind the scenes, as the pressure intensified, different people wobbled. In broadcasting, when lightening strikes, it strikes deep. For a time, no one is quite sure of you. You absorb the loneliness of power. Other people's doubts. You learn to be strong – or stronger than before it all happened. You acquire a very thick skin. So long as you are honest with yourself and the people around – you'll be alright. No one ever said that life is fair. If you are big enough to attack people you must be a big enough to take the hits back. To row with the punches.

1986 was a terrible year. Combustible. I was very nearly killed. There was a lot of very bad karma that year. It began well enough.

Traditionally, the Thursday night of the Conservative Party Conference was a party night for the BBC Outside Broadcast team who had spent ten weeks on the road covering the entirety of the conference season, from the TUC onwards. As a senior producer at the BBC, I usually stayed at the Grand Hotel in Brighton when one of the party conferences was taking place there. That year, however, 1986, the Tories were in the ascendancy. There was only room at the Inn for one member of the BBC staff – Sir Robin Day. I was to stay at the Metropole, next door. On that fateful night, I finished producing Sir Robin and David Dimbleby, wrapped up Newsnight's coverage, and headed for a late supper and a bit of partying. I was not a big party goer during the conference – I had to be up very early.

This night was different. I was expected to make an effort, to thank my teams. I had prepared everything for the big finale. The Prime Minister's speech. Thatcher was always good viewing. The party faithful loved her. I knew it would make good television. I was ready. And relaxed. After a fish supper in Wheelers on the front, I dropped into a few parties to say hello. I checked with my studio director that everything was ok for the following day. It was. At around 2.00am I decided to look in at the bar of the Grand Hotel and, if I could find someone interesting to talk to, have one final drink there. At 2.30 am I headed for my bed.

Twenty minutes later I put my head on the pillow at the Metropole. At 2.54, as I was drifting off, I heard an almighty explosion. The Brighton Bomb. The IRA had tried to kill Margaret Thatcher and half of her Cabinet. I was very proud of being British that night. The alarm went off in the hotel. Everyone trooped down the stairs as though it was all planned. There was no noise. No shrieking. The atmosphere was surreal. It was as though what was happening was entirely normal – a fire drill.

By now I was standing on the street outside of the Metropole. The bomb had ripped the guts out of the central pillar of the Grand Hotel. There was a huge amount of glass everywhere. Cabinet ministers were walking up and down, dazed. Pyjamas. Nightshirts. Blood. Glass. Disbelief. One of my abiding images is standing opposite the main entrance of the Grand and looking down into a pool of blood in which bits of glass had landed, catching the light – shimmering. As the arch lights of TV crews homed in on the shattered edifice next to it. In those days Ministers went about the conferences with little or no security. No longer.

With my superior sleeping through a lot of the first hour or so, I found myself in charge of the O.B. I was ushered into the back of the conference hall several times and ushered out several times. News – intelligence – came thick and fast. Often inaccurate. 'Margaret Thatcher has left Brighton.' 'Margaret Thatcher has returned.' 'Margaret Thatcher has a double – like Churchill.' 'Norman Tebbit is dead.' 'John Wakeham is dead.' So it went on. Then there was the spook. 'Mr Hogan we have got reason to believe that there is a bomb in these offices, what do you want us to do?' An easy one. 'Get out.'

And so we did, several times throughout the night.

At about 6.00am, sitting in front of a television monitor, I caught sight of Margaret Thatcher at the local police station. She never lost her poise. She never lost her instinct for the big occasion. She never lost her taste for danger either. In one way, she was in her element. And so was I. It was terrifying – an extraordinary night. Chaos reigned.

Outside the police station in Brighton that night, her instinct failed her for just a moment, as it was to do similarly in Paris some years later, when the game was up for her leadership. But that night I thought she was magnificent. When John Cole, the Northern Irish Political Editor of the BBC, saw her outside the police station he asked, sort of out of innocence, 'Will the conference go on Prime Minister?' At first she faltered. Then the fighting spirit that had driven Britain's first female Prime Minister, shone through. She grabbed the moment, not for the first or the last time, 'Yes! Yes! Yes! We go on.' Or words to that effect.

Three hours later, I sat in a half empty hall in the Brighton Conference Centre. 'Ladies and Gentleman. The Prime Minister.' On she walked. It was breakfast. It was raw. The morning after the night before. The half empty hall cheered. Their cheers echoed due to the fact that so few people were inside. Throughout the day victims and potential victims queued up to be interviewed – an endless stream of the shell shocked and bewildered. After endless hours of broadcasting to the world – it was immediately a world story – I arrived back in London, sickened but exhilarated. This was a huge event. Unique in British political history.

As I went back to London, I felt as though I had been raped – but survived. I went home and went to bed. It had been quite a day. The rest of the year kept up the pace. It was to be a helter skelter of emotion.

The weekend came and went. Then the holocaust. The other side fielded a brilliant and brutal barrister who ripped into us – painting a picture of us as a bunch of criminal minds that had conspired against a great party, to do it down, to destroy it.

The opening of the trial was a disaster for the BBC. There was to be no room for compromise, for debate, for a weighing up of the issues. No. This was to be a fight to the death. Suddenly we were on the run.

The BBC had to apologise and settle.

Walking back from the rooms of our barrister after what had been decided in private was a grim journey. The following day was worse. The public announcement. Scenes of jubilation from the other side. Watching the BBC Six O'clock News was painful. We were the lead story. We were at the centre of a perfect storm. With lightning lashing all around us.

In the weeks and months following the settlement of our legal case, I fought a very hard and lonely battle to claw my way back. I had to develop a very thick skin. I had to bottle up my feelings. I had to be strong for the people around me – at the BBC and at home. In the process I became even more self-reliant.

I received a lot of hate mail. One person writing to me told me Hitler was a very, very clever man. Another, that I should always look over my shoulder. They would get me – when I was least expecting it. Another said that they planned to string me up from a lamp post. Then there were the blades. One morning I was presented with a letter with blades carefully stuck to the line where I was expected to put my finger. And rip it along.

By 1989 I had re-established my career and role. As editor of 'This week, Next week,' my first network show, I wanted to buy up all the Sir David Frost interviews with the former Presidents of the United States. David famously led the successful bid for the breakfast television franchise years earlier – the TV AM Famous Five consortium – which included another friend of mine, with whom I had worked, Robert Kee.

I have always been drawn to unique people. Where TV is concerned, that means people who make an impact. As a teenager I fell in love with the Sir David Frost school of broadcasting and interviewing. David has always had a tremendous presence and sense of occasion on air – and off. He puts an enormous amount of preparation into his interviews – I believe he has done about 10,000. Above all he listens. He doesn't trample all over the interviewee – he relaxes them and draws them out. Then he pounces – but is never nasty. For my money he is one of the very best interviewers there has ever been. So when I became editor of This Week Next Week, with a very small budget, I wanted top quality at a price I could afford. I rang David, with whom I was to become great friends over the following years, and asked him if I could buy the right to a single showing of his interviews with past US Presidents – Nixon, Carter, Ford, Reagan. It was agreed. The audience loved it.

Before the programme came on air I was asked whether I would like to become TV AM's Political Editor. I turned it down, I am not an actor. Anyway, Adam Boulton, who took the job, is a truly gifted broadcaster and did the job much better than I could ever have done – and still does.

In recent years, I have hosted Adam for dinner during the Labour Party conference. I remember the scene very well. Adam arrives at 7.pm. He has a glass of wine; we have a fascinating discussion about the day's events. Come 7.50 – with the cameras and lights set up just outside where we are having dinner – he breaks off. 'Adam you are in vision. Cut and cue.' 'Well here at the Labour conference the knives have been out all day for the Prime Minister...' The same scenario is replayed at 8.50pm and 9.50pm. Adam never flinches. Never shows any sign of nerves. Never fluffs a line.

1987 was a big year in my life. After the downs, came the ups. I covered the 1987 General Election, which Labour was expected to win. I never believed that Labour would pull it off. The party was still very divided, certainly too divided to run the country in my view. It was still unravelling its own extremist tendency and some of the policies that went with it. On election night I was down at Labour Headquarters – all day, all night and well into the next day. The late Vincent Hanna – who had become the BBC's polling supremo – had convinced the Labour party and the BBC's election night team that Labour was going to be victorious. When the first results started to come in, for about an hour, it looked as though he was right. Then it all fell away very rapidly for Labour. New dawn turned into a dark nightmare.

The atmosphere was one of bereavement for what might have been. At about 4.00am, Adam Raphael, at the time the presenter of Newsnight, and I put our heads on wooden desks and drifted off to sleep. At about 8.00am I persuaded Peter Mandelson, the architect of the Labour campaign, that he should do what I think was his first interview – certainly since the result. He thought about it. Then said yes. It was a strange and surreal moment. Sitting behind his desk was a radiator on which sat a pair of white briefs. But Peter wasn't running up the white flag. He gave a cracking interview. Then Neil Kinnock arrived, having traveled down over night from Wales. It was a very sad moment. He and Glenys had worked tremendously hard. They had been full of hope. Up and down the country, people kept telling him that they were going to win. He went into a private meeting with the party faithful. For him, the sadness was that despite the gargantuan effort Labour had still been defeated. It wasn't a matter of ideology, more a case of wasted energy.

As luck would have it, I became the boss, the editor of virtually all the big names in News and Current Affairs. Among these was Sir Robin Day – the enfant terrible of broadcasting. Robin was a legend and an institution rolled into one. There is no doubt that he was – at his best – one of the very best interviewers. He was a star, of course. He was also very old hat. A bit coarse. Sexist. Frightened of women. Gentlemen's club. And brilliant. He could be half asleep in an interview and suddenly spring to life: 'What did you say? Repeat it.' The public and the politicians loved him. He liked me. And resented me a bit. I was young. He was old. I was on the way up. He was on the way down. I wasn't frightened of him.

I remember one morning at the Liberal Conference, Robin asked me why Cyril Smith wasn't there. The extraordinarily fat, yet charismatic liberal figure. I replied, 'I don't know. I'll call him.' Cyril, from Rochdale, said 'Lad, I'd be there but they don't have any baths in the rooms big enough to fit me.' Gold dust. I told Robin. So we broadcast this fact. It took off. It became a national story. No hotels with big enough baths for Cyril.

When I took over the reins in 1987, in charge of the party coverage, I was determined to change a lot of things. I love politics. Debate. But I couldn't bear the wasted opportunity of showing endless hours of very boring gavel to gavel coverage. You know the type of thing. A debate about clause 1(a) of the Highways Act. No. I decided to cut away. To big interviews. To reflect the growing importance of the fringe – where the real debate, the real power struggle, was taking place. Yet again this was a radical departure. I was attacked. I knew I would be. But I wanted to serve the audience.

That autumn I was made editor of 'This Week, Next Week,' The BBC's weekly political programme. I was to edit it until a permanent editor arrived with a large budget for its replacement, 'On The Record.' I seized the opportunity. I was nobody's stop-gap. With the show presented by Vivian White, the tallest man in broadcasting and a very clever one, we produced some of the best political interviews seen on British Television. We made front page news. The interviews which stood out at the time and stand out to me now are: the one in which Kinnock signalled, for the very first time, that he was dumping Labour's commitment to unilateral nuclear disarmament and Nigel Lawson's where, as Chancellor of the Exchequer, he revealed the depth of his seething dislike for the style and policies of Margaret Thatcher. There was a sense of history in the making. In both cases the person at the centre of the drama was somewhat overwhelmed by what was happening to them. It was as though events were driving them rather than the other way around.

I was riding high again. I was to be offered the deputy editorship of 'On The Record.' I turned it down. 'Ok. What about creating your own department, News events? You could look after our election coverage and the party conferences.' Later I would add documentaries and Question Time to my portfolio. I accepted the role gracefully and happily.

We made a lot of brilliant programmes under the News Events banner. However, our style and culture was different to the style and culture imposed on the BBC at that time. I was a publisher. I wanted to give the viewer the opportunity to hear the case, see the whole picture, and make his or her own mind up. I did not want to dictate. I was dealing with potentially dangerous stuff all the time. In the land of Thatcher versus Kinnock, British politics, like British society, was very potent and extremely polarised. But I did not intend to duck the issue or run away.

Around this time I discovered that I am very calm in a crisis. Two incidents stick in my mind. As editor of the BBC European Elections programme, I was in charge of a show that would cover the whole of Europe and last for five and a half hours. I had outside broadcast units dotted all over the place and a running order featuring literally hundreds of sequences. We rehearsed. And rehearsed. And rehearsed. The presenter, a genius of the genre, was David Dimbleby. In the run-up to the show going on air, as an experiment, someone took my blood pressure. 'It's amazing.' 'Why? 'It's amazing' came the reply. 'You would never know you are under any pressure at all. Not a peep.' Then there was the crisis. About ten minutes before we were due to go on air, at about 10.15pm, the man in charge of the vax computer which would spew out all of the election graphics came into the control room 'We have a problem. Errors have crept into the computer. 'Errors?' 'Some wrong information has been fed in.' 'Like a virus?' I enquired. 'Yes. Like a virus. What shall we do?' the man asked now sweating profusely, 'Go ahead?' 'No, of course not!' I snapped. 'Shut the computer down and reprogram it.' 'But you won't have any results,' he implored. 'Better that than the wrong results!' As I was deciding this I could see the previous TV show coming to a close. A quick word in David's ear. 'Here's the problem…I will tell you what to say …..We'll spend the first twenty minutes setting the scene. You interview the four studio guests…..OK Run Election titles.' 20 Seconds. 'OK David…'You say it's a night of lost seats for the Tories…' David Voice Over, 'A night of lost seats…' I was reading off the Press Association Wires, so I knew I was right to say this. 20 minutes later the computer was fixed. The show kicked in. No one noticed. No one complained.

As ever, in the midst of the controversy, daily life went on. In the October after the 1987 election my second child was born. Alexander James Hogan was born 30th October 1987 – An absolute delight. I had learnt my lesson from the birth of my daughter – don't take anything for granted. So when, during the Tory Party conference and the day before Margaret Thatcher's speech, my wife called me to say that the baby could be on the way, I took it very seriously. Had he been born that day he would have been ten weeks premature. Thankfully it was a false alarm, so I stayed at the conference and returned home later. The day and timing of his birth was the exact opposite of Cassie's. Alexander was born at five minutes to one in the afternoon – lunch time – on the quietest day of the year. The room in which he entered the world – at Queen Charlotte's Hospital in Stamford Brook, West London – was like a restaurant going bust. There was no one else there. Outside, it was the days of the 1987 storm. Trees falling to the ground everywhere. As with the wind, Alexander shot out of my wife's womb like a white tornado.

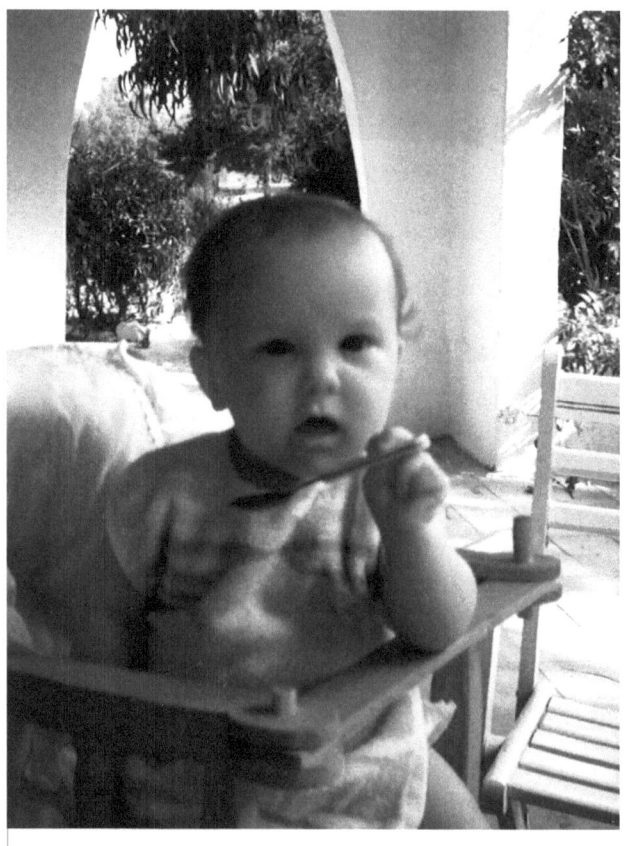

Alex

One of the abiding images in my life was when standing in the room where Alexander had just been born, my eyes travelled from his tiny, but perfect body, out of the window where a very old man who looked half as old as time was walking against the ferocious wind hardly making any progress. In my over active imagination I couldn't believe that he could have many days of life left in him. So one entered the world – all shiny and new, full of vitality. One left it – drained. Life and death.

Thanks to the success of News Events, the unit I set up inside BBC TV News and Current Affairs, I was also asked to look at covering the free elections in Romania following the fall of the communist bloc and the execution of Nicholas Ceausescu, the communist tyrant. It was the most dangerous trip of my life. The idea of pumping live elections results from these places was virtually unthinkable. But I thought 'fuck it.' We'll do it. I did deals left, right and centre. I gathered the best and brightest. Bucharest was the wild-west but Czechoslovakia was manageable. I situated David Dimbleby in a glass box which we built next to the statue of King Wenchlaus. Planted Peter Snow and his election night graphics on a balcony overlooking the square. And invited Paul Simon of Simon and Garfunkel who was playing in the square to appear on the show. It was a huge success. The official history of the BBC year – the Governor's Report-recognised the achievement of all involved.

Czech elections

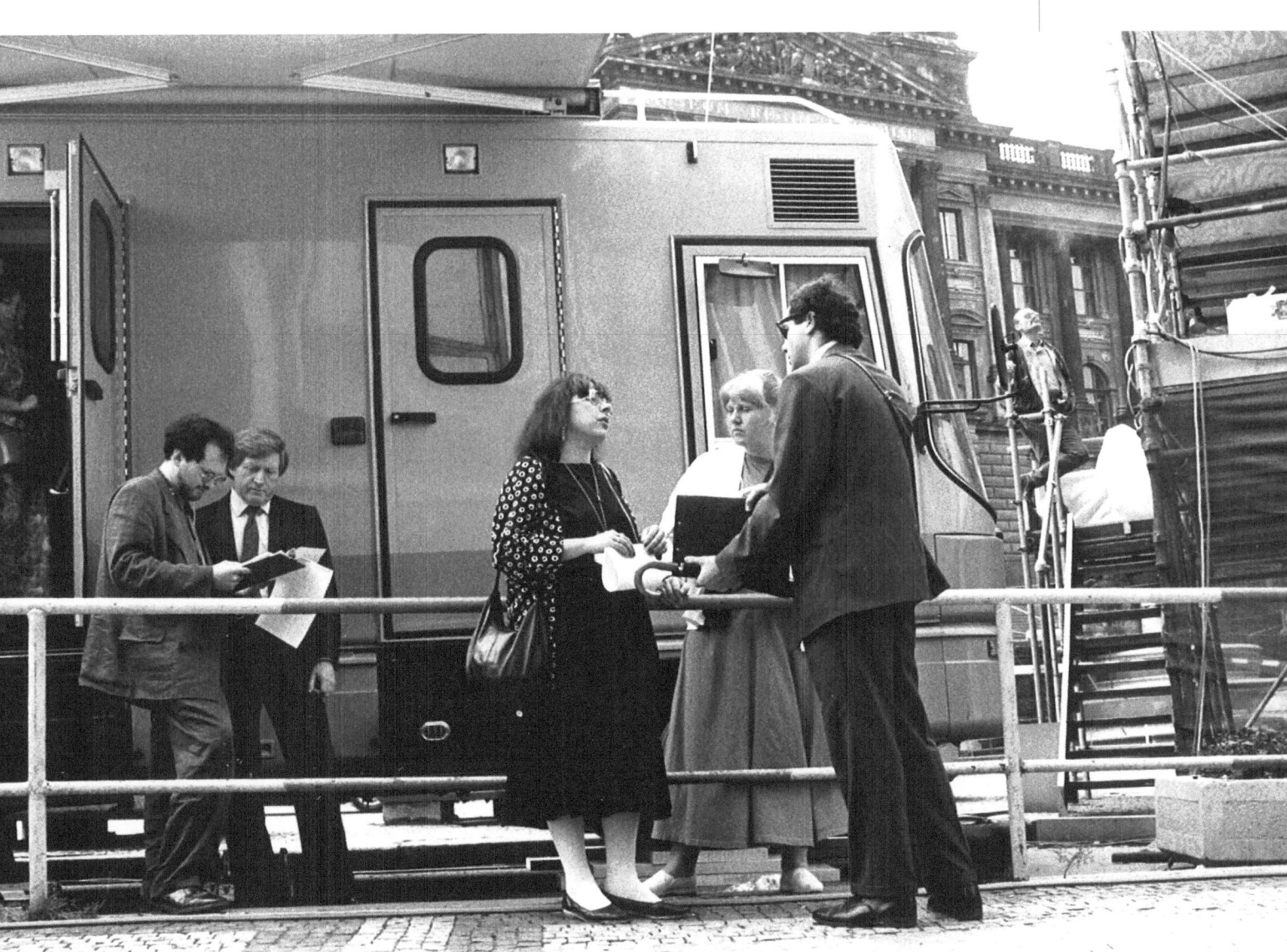

There were times when I did not think that I would get out alive. It was also a very moving, remarkable and, at times, hilarious experience. I flew from Prague to Bucharest on Terom Airlines – a pretty terrifying experience in its own right. The airplane did not land so much as fall out of the sky – with a violent plunge. Once it settled, I could see that we were going to have visitors. A stream of troops and tanks drove up to the plane. As we alighted we were reminded, if we needed reminding, that we had landed into the scene of a bloody and violent revolution. Everywhere you could hear gunfire – some close, some distant. The buildings were shot to ribbons. I had rifles stuck up my nose. All I could think of saying was, 'We're BBC,' as though everything should stop for me.

We were met at the airport by a guide – provided for us by I forget whom but the security services of some sort. He would look after us. Show us around. Get us in and out of restaurants, that sort of thing. We travelled to the Europa Hotel. As I went up in the lift a very young boy put his hand on my crotch, 'You have dollars?' The Europa was the hotel that had been attacked heavily during the fall and execution of Ceausescu. It was also by repute a bit of a honey trap for foreign nationals. I went and looked at my room. The bed head was covered in gun-shot holes. The balcony had been hit so many times it was hard to believe that it had not shattered altogether. Then a knock on my door. A colleague. 'James darling there is a couple in my room.' I walked along the corridor, lent on the door and burst in. There a totally naked couple, a man and a woman, were fully and deeply engaged in intercourse – a pursuit they showed no sign of giving up on until we got someone up from reception to break up the party.

We were there on a mission. So the following day we set about our business. There followed a day of incidents and extraordinary sights. As we left the hotel, by foot, we bumped into a shepherd standing with his sheep outside the hotel – the main hotel in Bucharest. Up a side street we witnessed a long queue of people lined up in front of a skip, full of soil, from which a man plucked potatoes for sale. Then we got in a car with our guide. We visited Ceausescu's Bucharest home where he and his wife, Helena, were arrested. The place was modern, chalet style, and shot to ribbons. Then on to the palace Ceausescu had built for himself – all lumps of dark oak and marble. We were told he was paying for it by turning down the heat in the whole country, channelling the savings to the project. We were also told that he had over 40 homes in different parts of the country, some of which he had not even visited. That night, to the sound of gunfire, we walked past the headquarters of the Romanian Secret Service, the Securitate. A spooky place by day and even spookier by night. Then there was a visit to the opera. As my guide settled me into a box and just before the performance was about to start, he tapped me on the shoulder 'You know who's seat you are sitting in?' 'No.' 'Ceausescu's.' It was not a comfortable evening.

But still we hadn't done what we had come to do – the recce. We needed to find a place to stage the programme. 'What about the military HQ?' The next day I ventured to the site. Huge rows of tanks. Huge number of soldiers. Rifles shoved in my face. Aggression. Nerves. Instability. I blagged my way passed it all. Muttering 'BBC, BBC, BBC.' The BBC is the biggest brand worldwide where news is concerned. It opens every door. Confronted by the man running the whole shooting match – in every sense – I suddenly realised the risk I was taking. I was so determined to do my job, I had forgotten – for the moment – that this was not a TV or movie set. This was real. A lot of people were very frightened. There were bullets flying. No one knew or cared who I was. They were caught up in their own drama. Their own reality.

Anarchic. This was no place to be building a studio. Deploying an outside broadcast unit. This wasn't Aintree. The Grand National. Nor was it Prague. Czechoslovakia was a piece of cake by comparison. No. This was the wild west. I phoned back to Television Centre. We must give Romania a miss. And concentrate our resources on the Czech Elections.

We had nearly been killed several times in Bucharest, despite the best endeavours of our guide. At one point we were hustled inside a bookshop to take cover from overhead fire. Walked at speed through the front of the shop, which looked like something out of the 1940s, we were taken down, down, to the basement deep underground. The same day, the day before we were due to leave to go back home, we visited a similarly appointed establishment, this time a makeshift art gallery. I wanted to buy a piece of Romanian art. I got my guide to help. I chose a painting, just a small oil painting, but a beautiful one, that had been painted a couple weeks before. It was of a very English looking gentleman sitting in a deck chair on a tennis court reading a newspaper. I was enthralled. I couldn't believe that something so calm could have been painted in the midst of all this mayhem. I bought it paying the equivalent of £120. In those days – or in Ceausescu's day – I was told they chopped off your hands if you tried to take an oil painting out of the country. The painting had to be concealed. When it came to leaving the country, and going through security, I was asked 'Are you taking anything back with you?' 'What is this?' 'A painting.' 'A painting?' 'It's just a little present. 'A present?' My inquisitor was distracted. He let me through. I felt like a drug mule that had gotten away. I will never forget the relief I felt when we finally got out of Bucharest.

In some of my darkest hours around this time, I felt that I was at the centre of the struggle between good and evil. I absorbed the violence of the Brighton Bomb and felt violated. I saw a lot of blood spilt that night. I absorbed the terror then – and when I travelled to Eastern Europe. I anticipated the ethnic cleansing that was to follow the collapse of the soviet bloc. After all I had witnessed its equivalent in Bucharest where Ceauşescu uprooted whole villages and paraded the spoils in the centre of the city – the scalps of a brutal collectivisation. To this extent the 'Eclipse' series anticipates the 'Blood' paintings in my work.

When the call came offering me Question Time, I was in Bucharest. Would I become editor of Question Time? 'You bet!' Question Time was the biggest brand in News & Current Affairs. I would agree to edit Question Time but there would be conditions. 'Conditions?' 'Yes conditions.' 'What do you want?' 'I want a proper budget. I want to take the programme around the country. I want the audience to be scientifically composed – and, oh yes I want to go live.' From now on we would make news. We would be at the heart of the political agenda.

So the deed was done. It was a remarkable throw of the dice. For a start there was the fall of Margaret Thatcher. Then there was the Gulf War.

The fall of Margaret Thatcher was a broadcaster's gift. The resignation speech of Sir Geoffrey Howe, Thatcher's Chancellor and Foreign Secretary, was the killer blow. I called a series of former Prime Ministers and senior politicians personally. 'Ted will you come?" Of course he would. He always hated Thatcher. Jim Callaghan, a prickly character at the best of times, 'Jim, will you do it? Yes?' Enoch Powell – 'Yes'…And so it went on. I rang Television Centre. We had an abundance of riches. Could we have a second show? Frantic calls. 'Yes. Yes. Do it.' They were two great shows. The presenter, Peter Sissons, was on sparkling form. In the green room afterwards, I had some fascinating conversations. That night rumours swirled around Westminster that John Major, a surprising choice, was emerging as the front-runner to succeed Thatcher. Hearing this, I said to Heath, 'Don't you think he's a bit ordinary?' He replied, 'Ordinary! Ordinary! She's Ordinary. She's never written a piece of music, never sailed a yacht.' That was the criteria of hatred. The start of the first Gulf War offered an opportunity for more of the same. When we came off air – we stood together in the green room watching CNN where, the presenter was wearing a gas mask. Echoes of the Second World War or may be premonitions of a Third World War.

I was determined to make Question Time real, relevant. I wanted it to return it to the heart of events. The Gulf war was the opportunity. The former Tory Prime Minister, Sir Edward Heath had very controversially gone to visit Sadam Hussein in Baghdad. I phoned him in Baghdad. 'Ted, if you want it, I will make you the centre piece of Question Time – BBC1 – for a whole hour? If you do Newsnight you will be lucky to get ten minutes.' Ted had famously once said of LWT's Weekend World that after you deducted the commercials and Brian Walden's questions you were lucky if you got five minutes on air. It was agreed. Ted flew back to London into a storm of publicity. 'No, No I can't speak to BBC News. No, No I can't speak to ITN. I have promised Question Time that I would speak there first.' Electric.

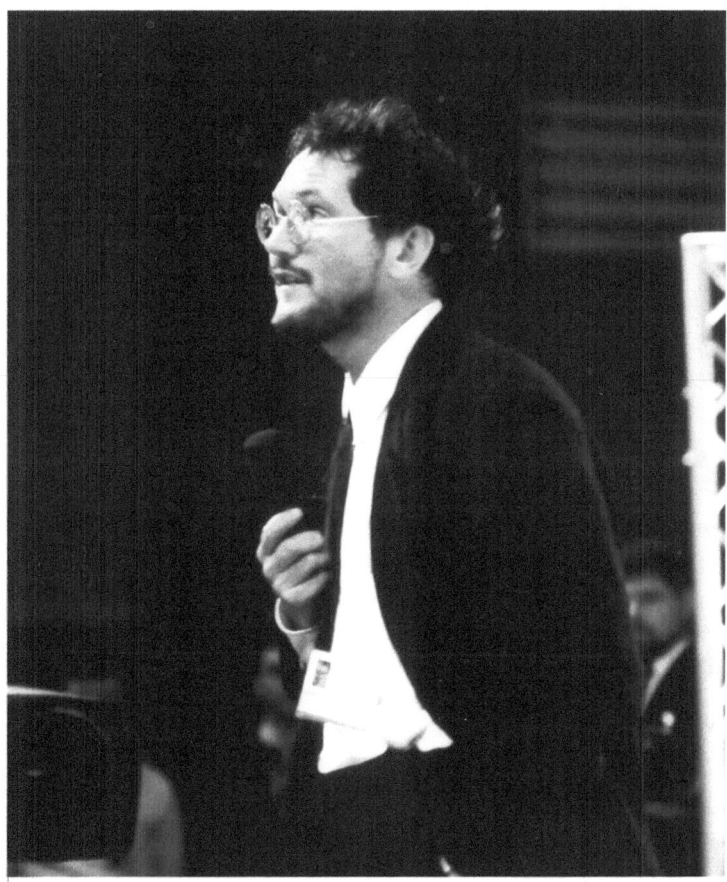

Warming up the audience at Question Time

When Ted appeared he was hot. He was under pressure. Then came the allegations from the audience: 'You are a traitor Sir! Ted lent over and smashed the beautifully crafted glass table that I had designed replacing the old wooden one. Jesus I thought. He is going to smash it to pieces. He was angry to say the least. 'How dare you challenge my sincerity, my loyalty?' The place erupted. Mercifully the table stayed intact.

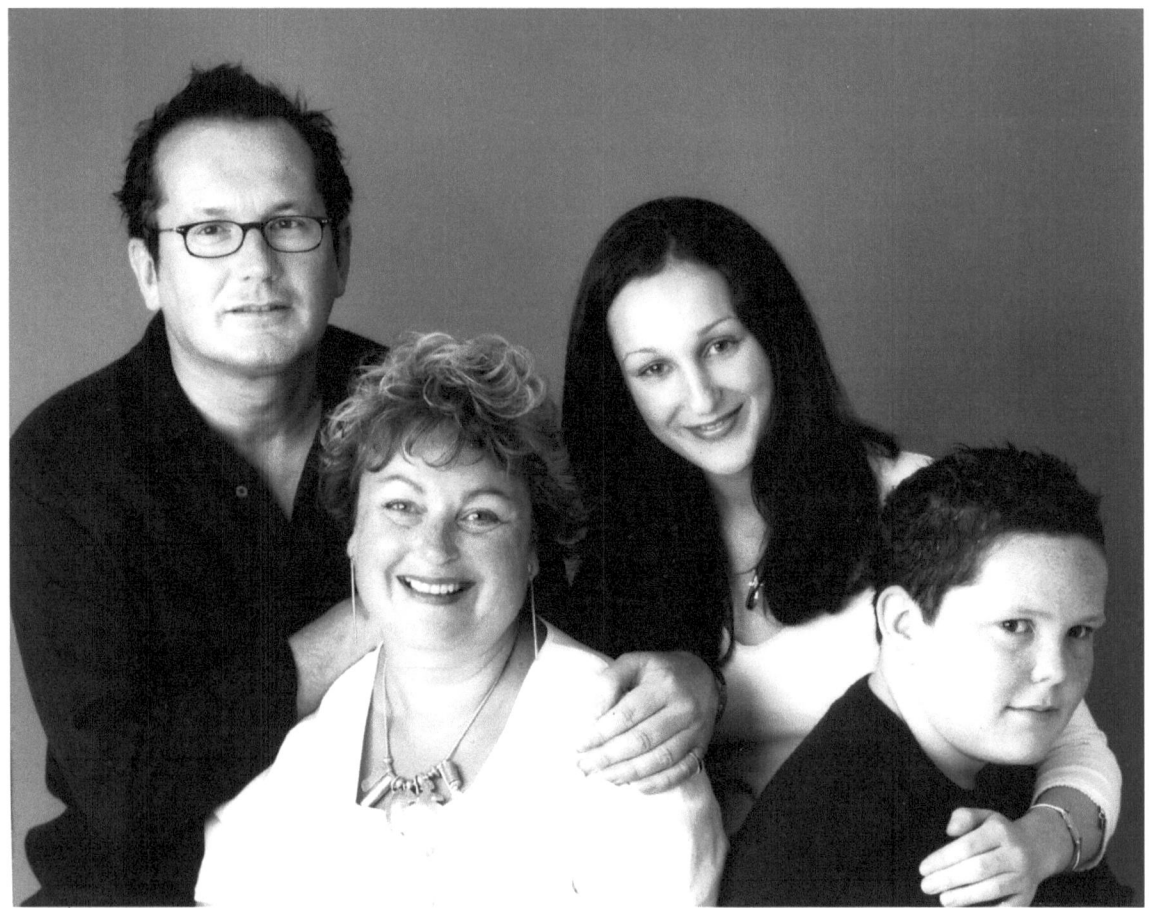

My Family 2001

By now Cassie was on her way to Oxford and Alexander was studying at Kingston Grammar School. We celebrated our 50th birthdays and our 25th wedding anniversary in 2001.

At the end of the Gulf War, enter the first Charles Denton – I have been enormously privileged to have met two Charles Dentons in my life, the first a genius of TV – the other a great enthusiast and supporter of my work. Charles the TV man was brave. Charles was a publisher by instinct. We got on famously. Charles had fought tooth and nail to bring Inspector Morse and Spitting Image to our screens. He now ran what was at the time, 1992, the most powerful independent television production company in the UK. One of the new breed that had grown up following the creation of Channel 4 and the introduction of the rule that the likes of BBC and ITV would have to buy in 25% of their programmes from the Indies.

As head of Zenith, Charles had written the programming section of the Carlton TV application for the London franchise. Zenith was owned 51% by Carlton, 49% by Paramount. Charles asked me if I would like to become Managing Director of Zenith's newly planned Factual Programming Division. I said yes. Along the way, before I left the BBC, I linked up with Zenith to bid for the contract to produce Question Time running it as an independent. The BBC had decided to privatise the show to comply with the quota.

The early nineties were a difficult time for the UK economy and for the television industry. Running an independent firm is always difficult. They are truly among the most difficult businesses to manage, albeit fascinating. Not long after I joined Zenith, I was asked whether I would like to become a fellow of the London School of Economics. The idea was that I would become the Robert McKenzie fellow with special reference to the television and film industry for two years. It would give me the opportunity to write about what was happening in television – the economics of independent production and the power relationship between the independents and the still almighty broadcasters. Once again I just could not resist. And went onto to write 'From Demigods to Democrats – The Television Revolution, 1976 to 1996.' Running two commercial television companies by day and researching and writing by night was very hard but I am glad I did it. While I was at LSE I was also involved with the running of SelecTV the comedy and drama house for whom I led the Channel5 bid.

Along the way another disaster of sorts came my way. The first Charles Denton felt aggrieved that Zenith did not have any share of the rights income when it made a successful show – and it made a lot. Zenith was simply paid for making the shows. Inspector Morse was not only hugely popular and successful; it created a whole new genre which many people thought could never be pulled off. It was to be a two hour

TV drama – like a film – and shown in peak time. It was a risk but it worked. However, all revenues went to the owners of the production company – Carlton. The scene was set for an almighty bust up. And we got one. Charles and Michael Green – owner of Zenith and Carlton TV – had had a row to end all rows. Despite winning the London TV licence, Zenith would not be making Carlton TV programmes after all. The logic for my move had just evaporated.

Despite this, I didn't feel too despondent. The LSE work was interesting. And I always believed that something would turn up. Which it did. A very nice man called John Hall, who had just bought Zenith, had been thinking about me. 'Your CV is fantastic. You could be director general.' I thanked him but told him that I didn't have any ambitions in that direction. 'I think you will get on with Alan McKeown. He knows all about talent. You would like each other.' I didn't know Alan but I knew of him. Alan was the truly gifted television producer who produced programmes such as *Auf Wiedersehen Pet, Birds of A Feather, Goodnight Sweetheart, Lovejoy,* and *Love Hurts*. He pioneered the genre. And he was one of the very first people in the TV industry to understand the importance of owning the rights to the programmes you make. He was fun. He was married to Tracey Ullman. A huge star in America. Alan bought out the division of Zenith that I had created. I joined his team in Derby Street in Mayfair. This was in 1994. The TV industry, having been in the doldrums, was picking up a bit. The early signs of a lift in the stock market were beginning to surface. Alan and I hatched a plan.

Alan had reversed SelecTV into a shell owned by the late Robert Maxwell. It was listed on the London Stock Exchange. We would use SelecTV as the bid vehicle for an audacious attempt to win the upcoming Channel5 license. Alan had a good track record where winning licenses was concerned. SelecTV had joined forces with Clive Hollick to bid, successfully, for the new South of England franchise, Meridian. SelecTV became a 15% stakeholder. Similarly Alan had helped the late David English of DMGT to secure one of the new cable licenses in London to produce London Regional News. Alan and I were aware that it would be a tall order to land Channel5, but it was worth a try. In the event we very nearly pulled it off. We were pipped to the post by Greg Dyke – who was to become a great friend of mine – and the Pearson consortium. I always thought Pearson would get the license, but I do not regret trying. I learnt a vast amount about business in a very short period of time. Weeks and months spent with lawyers and bankers teaches you very fast. I was eager to learn and attended every single meeting. I was ready to take my next step – which would be into the City.

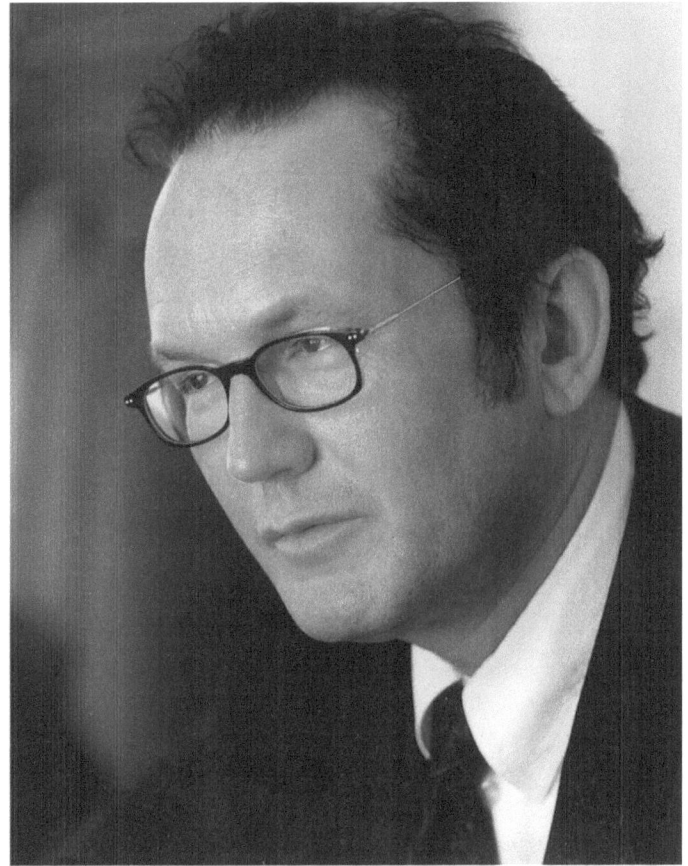

PR man

Standing back from my time as an independent producer, my overwhelming sensation and memory of those days is the total lack of power that independents have in relation to the broadcasters. While there are some notable exceptions to this rule – Simon Cowell etc-it is still the case and probably always will be. The atmosphere in the TV industry in the early 90's was the same as today. There were only three primary buyers – BBC, ITV, and C4. Huge amounts of work went into creating ideas. Formats. Many were stolen. Very few commissioned. Indies were the equivalent of casual labourers. They resembled the pathetic dockers in *On The Waterfront*.

The chill wind of hard economic reality blew through the corridors of the Indies like a hurricane, in stark contrast to the climate inside the Broadcasters, which remained warm and comfortable. Some comments taken from my LSE research sum up the situation very well indeed and are as relevant today as they were back in the mid-nineties. David Elstein – Ex ITV & BSKYB – 'It is in the interests of the tiger to have deer for lunch.

That is the nature of the industry, not to encourage deer to grow horns and sharp teeth and sharp hooves and indeed eighty miles an hour running speeds. Tigers would not flourish.' At the other end of the scale, one independent told me his only ambition in life was 'to cease being a prostitute to circumstance.'

In 1996 I left TV and became a PR man. Once again I was attracted to ground-breaking enterprises, at first Brunswick, the corporate communications company, then College Hill. Both very creative and entrepreneurial. Both willing to innovate and take risk.

Around the time of these events I had one of the most frightening experiences of my life. Unheralded. One morning I couldn't get out of bed. I wasn't depressed; I just had no energy whatsoever. It was as if a vampire had entered my room during the night and sucked all the lifeblood out of my body. I suddenly looked very pale, very down, very ill. Some days I could barley muster the energy to walk. I dragged myself through the daily routine teetering on the edge of despair. My job demands a public presence. There was no escape. So I gathered up what strength I had and made myself work through. Even giving speeches. In truth I felt as though I would shortly collapse or cave in as the life blood drained from my body. I prayed for a cure to an illness that I did not understand. Couldn't tackle because I did not know what I was tackling. Couldn't fight because I did not know how to fight it. People close to me started to worry. I started to worry. For weeks but for what seemed a lifetime I struggled to find a fix, a cure, or at least a reason. I visited my GP on numerous occasions and visited a psychiatrist – not once but several times.

When it happened it happened upon me. I was frightened to go to sleep. Frightened not to go to sleep. The blood slipped from me as it had done from my father and my mother. My skin turned urine yellow. My flesh stone white. I peered out – looking in, looking beyond. I waved. I drowned. I hoped for death. Or at least some release. I wasn't scared only resigned. I thought the game was up. When your parents die so terribly young you are either not surprised by early death or you anticipate it. Some people crave it. I did none of these things. I was simply all at sea. When I went to see a psychiatrist – a gifted man – he said you seem a bit flat, a bit low. I don't think you have ever allowed anyone to see you like that since your parents died. I told him he was right. Another friend of mine who died too young around this time told me 'you never let go'. I agreed. The connections are obvious; but they weren't to me at the time.

You always learn things when confronted by personal tragedy. Or in this case a near death experience. My psychiatrist explained to me the inner workings of the human brain; as we in the West at this stage of our evolution – understand it. 'You see' he said 'the brain works on electricity. Information is conveyed from A to B to C. The problem is if you are unhappy, or simply dysfunctional, the information gets trapped at B. You can't move forward. Can't process. You become anxious. You become depressed. You can't sleep. You go to sleep for a couple of hours. Wake up as though it was the middle of the day. Dawn and afternoon are one. You start to terrorise yourself. You begin to eat yourself. You are your own worst enemy.'

He told me certain aspects of the way the brain works are entirely mechanical. 'You have taken too much pain,' he said. 'But you can deal with it-process it' How? He sent me to one of his colleagues. She specialised in obliteration. She told me that there was a better way than always supporting everyone around – doing all the heavy lifting, always. She told me about a psychiatrist who had a patient – disturbed – who rode on horseback through the tree –lined avenues characteristic of France. As the patient rode on, faster, faster, faster; as the trees cut, cut, cut, like a movie in front of her eyes so the memory, the pain, dissipated. So that she was free of the pain and could live in the present. So we rocked together, simulating the ride, washing away some of the memories. To my amazement it worked. Not entirely. But largely.

I was so desperate I remember wishing I had cancer – for me, with my family history, a terrible thing to hope for. At least if it was cancer, I would know what it was. What I was dealing with. Just when I thought it would never get any better, I got a diagnosis and some medication. My doctor told me it was not an accident that I had become ill at the age of 49 – which I was at the time. This was the age at which my mother had died.. 'So what is it?' 'You are suffering from survivor guilt. People who work in the armed forces are very familiar with the syndrome.' I was replicating my mother's illness. I was feeling that I did not deserve to outlive her. It made sense to me. As soon as I knew, I started to get better. No matter how bad things get nothing will ever be as bad or as frightening as this period.

As a PR Man I have observed the loneliness of power and come to value the independent spirit even more. It is very tough running big organizations that are going through a transformation. Thus the people I have advised and for whom I have the greatest admiration are Bob Ayling, who ran British Airways and now chairs various companies and Greg Dyke, the former Director of the BBC. They are resilient.

They are brave. They never give up. Above all they are true to themselves and to their values. Like me, they have had their ups and downs – famously – but through it all they kept a sense of proportion. And stuck to the task. When they were denounced they didn't bleat or retreat – they fought. When the crisis passed – they moved on. It wasn't easy for either of them – or for me – but they did it. In many ways they are more trusted and admired than at the beginning.

Before I leave this chapter, I will add one more thing. The tragedy of my parents' death and the struggle that ensued strengthened me and my brothers and sisters. It was incredibly tough – yes. But it did not defeat any of us. There was to be a happy ending. My eldest sister, Valerie, deserves a lot of the credit. She remains the centre of the family. Through thick and thin she inspires a sense of optimism. Her own children are very successful. One is a journalist, one an academic, one a doctor, one a PR man. Today she is a proud grandmother. My other brothers and sisters are also happy parents. For me there was a landing also. I am incredibly proud of my two children. They too think for themselves. The independent spirit lives on.

There was no warning. When I awoke at the start of 2007 it could have been an ordinary day. It wasn't. I could have woken up blind. I didn't. I woke up to bright colours. I dream in colour. Everything was very vivid. A host of images came flooding into my head. It was as though a force had blown open a box of tricks, a box of colours. A switch had been thrown. Thereafter my life would change.

So my art took over. It marked the end of a chapter in my life and the start of another. My art would connect my heart and my soul through the medium of paint.

Paint is very odd. God is in it somewhere. Mixing it up. Sparking something, connecting. It's hard to explain. He takes over sometimes. Sometimes leaves you adrift. A bit like paint itself. Who could have anticipated such a thing?

Almost without knowing what I was doing or where I was going, I headed for Covent Garden to the London Graphic Centre. I was very excited. More than excited, thrilled. Row and rows of paint – of every hue. Dozens of different whites. Different greens. Different blues…dozens of brushes. Dozens of knives. Canvases to the left and right. Some square. Some rectangular. Some big. Some small. Some huge. Chemical concoctions – white spirit. Linseed oil. Turpentine. I was a nobody in the art world – or even in the art shop. Yet I was welcomed with open arms simply because I had a need to paint and the guts to try. A lovely man called Matthew took me under his wing. I was initiated. He steered me to Michael Harding's paint. Hand-made earth tones. It is the best paint. Only one problem they don't make gold or silver. They aren't true colours. Even so, I love them both and use a lot of them in my work. So I would use Windsor & Newton to fill the gap.

All the memories of painting as a child came racing back. It was a very sensual experience. Very physical. Very natural. I re-lived the smells of childhood associated with paint, only this time it was much more potent. Instead of the aroma of water-colour, this time it was the real thing, the power of oil. Immediately I added to the mix various industrial strength chemicals which produced an even more heady brew. Yacht varnish, bleach, metal paint, iron filings, plaster, Cornish sand. The smells were overwhelming. They produced in me an almost psychedelic effect. What went on the canvas stimulated in me a visual and sensory response. No longer 2-D but 3-D.

As I painted I became more and more involved. After many hours of painting, having completed a canvas, I would get up in the middle of the night and re-work it. Adding more paint, more ingredients. I would re-visit the studio at the top of the house at various times to stare again at what I had done. Touching. Smelling. Feeling. Sometimes I would fire the canvas burning the oil paint to create a further chemical reaction. This produces a magical effect as well as an amazing mess. Fascinated by this process, I experimented with melting plaster on the canvas…I lost myself in the work. The hours flew by. I felt an overwhelming sense of joy. The meaning of human happiness. The delight of beauty.

THE ART UPSTART

People are like water – they find their own level. At some point in your life, you have to break free. You have to do something for yourself. If you duck it, you die long before you die. Not for nothing did Henry David Thoreau write, "The mass of men lead lives of quiet desperation". The haunting word is "quiet". As John Milton observed "The mind is its own place". The hand of God is something above and beyond. If you feel it, it will lead you places. That is how it has always been for me. So too with my art.

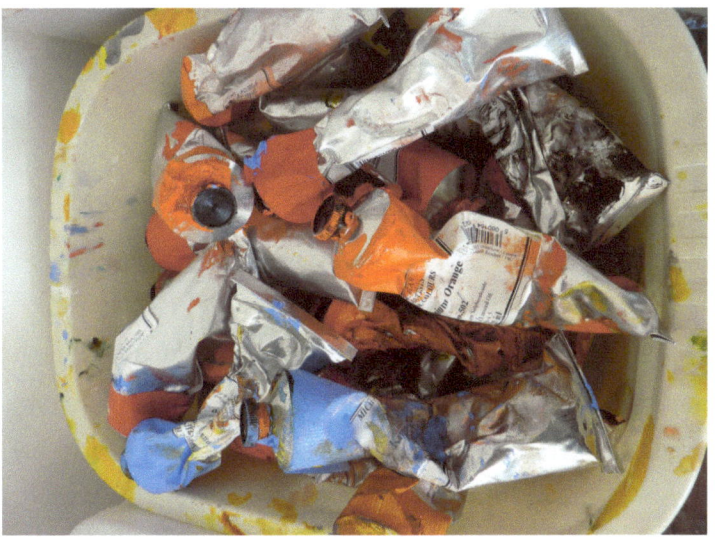

This is how it all started up again. One day, the start of January 2007. Out of the blue I started to paint again. It was as though I had never stopped. Taking up the knife was the most natural thing in the world. Looking back, I am amazed I ever stopped.

The mystery isn't that I went back. The chronology is pretty clear cut. I awoke with the thirst of someone in the desert. I didn't know what was happening to me but I knew what I had to do. Suddenly my lifeblood came flooding in to my head. There was a rush of colour and God's light. Tubes of paint. An eruption. I didn't have time to assess what was going on. I was simply propelled forward. The colours of the rainbow illuminated my senses. My soul was lit up. The feeling was over-powering. It didn't matter what other people said. I didn't care about rejection. I became more driven than ever. I grabbed hold of the paint like a man possessed. It was the start of a whole new chapter in my life.

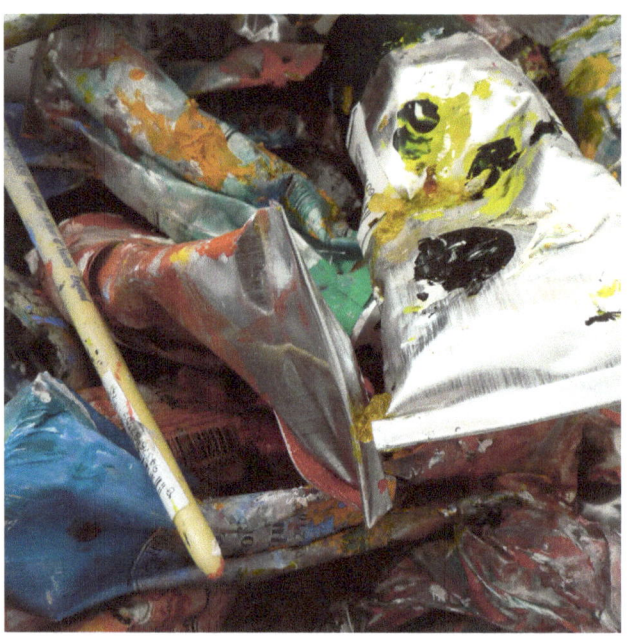

From the very start I had fixed ideas about what I did want to do and what I did not. I wanted to be an independent artist. I wanted to develop my own voice and style. I wanted to speak directly to the public. To anyone who was willing to give me a try. I did not want to be taught. I did not want to go through the system. I did not want to enter competitions. I did not want my work diluted. I did not want my pictures hung with anyone else's. I did want a one-man show.

From the very first day I went back to painting I always intended to have a one-man show and work towards it. I remember telling a friend this. To which they replied – 'You? – a one-man show?' 'Yes,' I answered, 'Why not?'. Came the reply, 'I don't know really.'

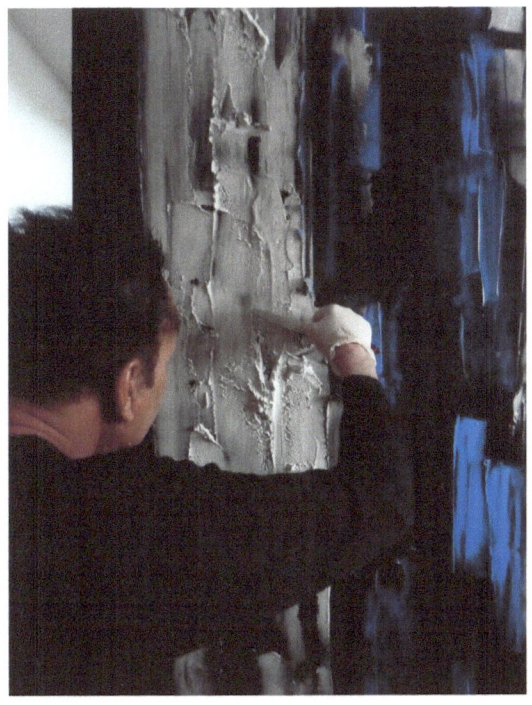

So at first I hatched a plan inside my head. Which is where it stayed from 2007 to the spring of 2009. Throughout this period and up to today, I worked seven days a week for four years. I worked my socks off in the city – which I still do and still love – And every weekend and every holiday on my art. By the spring of 2008 I was becoming sufficiently confident to start showing some people my work. That's always the first step. And a nerve racking one. Up until then only my wife and children had seen what I was doing. The paintings were locked away in a warehouse from prying eyes.

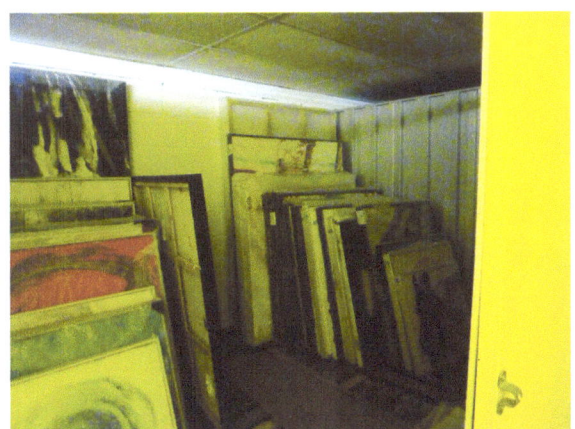

Some key moments came back to me. I showed a friend of mine who is very interested in art. And who has very good taste. I took a picture of **Dialectic I** and showed it to him. I said to him, 'I like it but you may think it is rubbish.' 'No,' he said 'it is not rubbish.' Then there was my dear friend, the late Ewen Balfour, a man devoted to the Arts – the former director of Corporate Affairs at the Royal Opera House. He had heard me speak about my art and requested that I bring in my portfolio for him to review. We were both partners at Brunswick the corporate communications company. So I agreed.

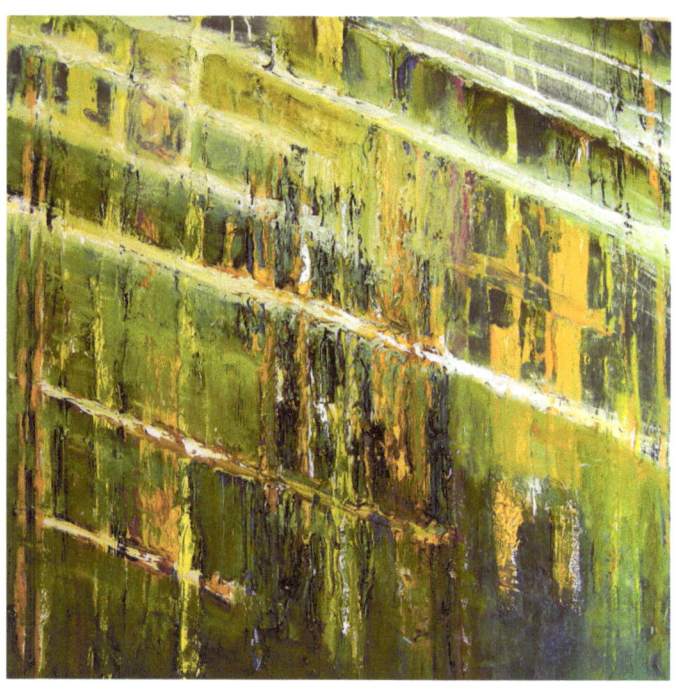

Ewen spent his life visiting galleries, museums, opera houses and events all over the world. We were immensely fond of each other. But I made him make a promise – be honest. I handed over the portfolio to him at the beginning of May 2008. He took it away to one of the meeting rooms. I gave it to him at 10.00 am. He did not emerge until 12.00pm. 'Well?' I asked. 'I had no idea you could do this. I would be delighted to own any one of them. And hang them on my wall. This art is what you will be remembered for.' He persuaded me to show the portfolio to another mutual friend, the former Liver Birds actress with whom we both worked at Brunswick we both liked and respected each other's judgement, Polly James. She thought they were fantastic, 'But how on earth do you get the time?' I explained I only do two things, the day job and the art. I don't have the time for anything else.

So I was encouraged from the beginning.

Gradually I started to share sight of the portfolio with other people for whom I have a great deal of respect. 2009. One big moment that summer was when I presented my work to the lovely man who runs the Redfern Gallery in Cork Street, Richard Selby. Richard had introduced me to the work of Paul Feiler in 1997 – a key influence. I took Richard and my wife to the Savile Club where I am a member and where beautiful paintings are housed including the work of Ben Nicholson – another favourite. After lunch we sat on the terrace as Richard read every word of the concise story and scrutinised every painting. My heart was in my mouth. He was someone who really knew about my type of art. Someone who makes a living out of selling it. As he leafed through, I became more relaxed. 'I love this one. And this one. That's a very strong painting. So is that. That's very powerful. Thought provoking...' Idiosyncratic 'Are there any you don't like?' I asked. 'Not really. No.' 'Have I got a chance do you think,' I followed up. 'A completely unknown artist?' 'Oh yes. Most definitely. I will help. I will show them to my directors. You can always call on me for advice.' A big moment.

So it was that things bubbled away that summer. As I received this private encouragement I drove myself on. Over the bank holiday weekend in August I locked myself away in the studio for four whole days. Never seeing anyone. My wife had gone to France for a short holiday. And to get away from my obsession. Over those four days I painted non-stop. Potent paintings. Not suited to the living room wall but, like so many of the big occasions in my life, something that I simply had to do.

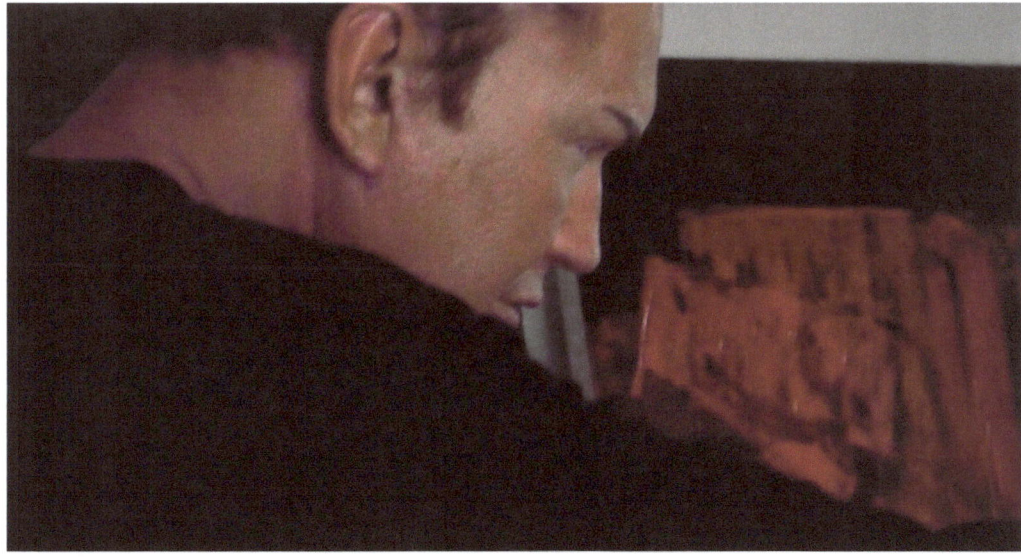

By August 2009, I was crystal clear that I would hold a one man show. Ignorance is bliss. If I had known more about the way the art world currently works or about the volume of work it entailed or about the amount of money you need – I would have been very scared – may be even scared off. But I knew nothing about those things. So, I raced forward.

I started to think about how I could do it all. I reflected on the fact that I understand the way the modern world of media works. I started to think about how a completely unknown artist – an upstart – could gain traction. Could reach out to people. Maybe people who felt excluded from the esoteric of the traditional art world. The question excited me. As the answer formulated I became very excited. And so did some of my friends. Around this time, I received yet more encouragement from a lovely man, the Finance Director and founder of Brunswick, Andrew Fenwick. I showed him my portfolio. He is a special man. And he sensed something special in the work. Wrongly people often think that people who are good with numbers cannot see art. Mathematics is beautiful.

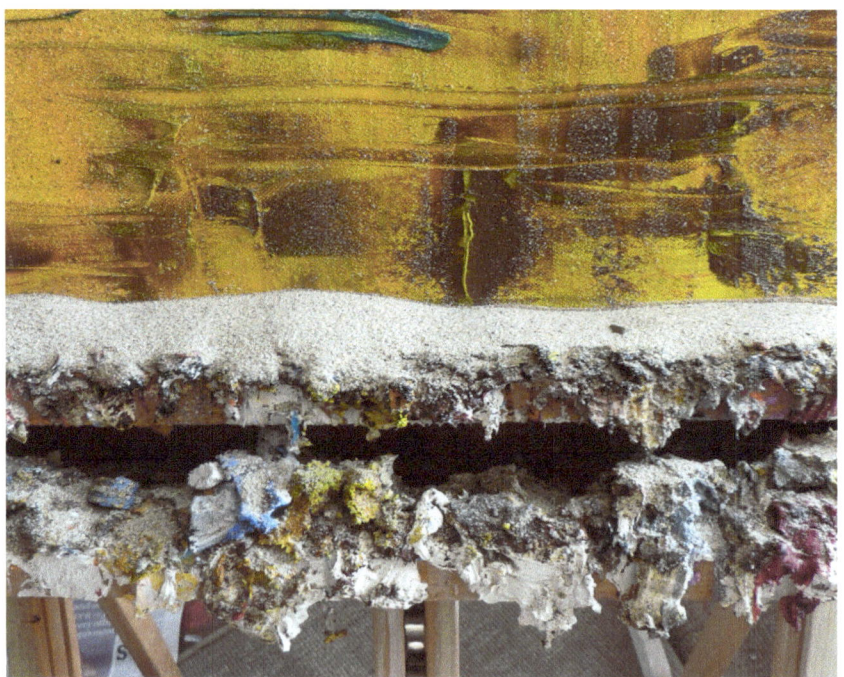

As I reflected on the way that digital communication are changing the world, I started to hatch a plan. I was very well positioned to do so as a PR man and an expert in all things related to media. I thought why not reach out across the globe to anyone who is interested in art. Show them what I am doing. Let them in. Allow them to share the work. Share in the struggle. They would not have to be rich; they wouldn't have to be dealers. They would be decent and ordinary people who happen to love art or happen to have an opinion. They would become my self-selected, self-elected, community of followers. Some would-be artists. Some enthusiasts. Some critics. There would be a dynamic.

The idea appealed to me because I was starting from scratch. Having a go. Before I signed off on the idea entirely, I went to various galleries and exhibitions. Two abiding memories. For the ordinary person going into a Mayfair gallery is a daunting experience. They almost certainly wouldn't go in at all. There is an air of the esoteric about many of these establishments. Similarly with exhibitions. And contemporary art. When I went to the Turner Exhibition in the autumn of 2009, I was struck by the most unlikely piece of art around which everyone was huddled – the Notice Board on which people were able to have their say – most of it negative, despairingly. The complaints were by, far the most compelling expression of the People's Art. A reaction to being excluded. To being taken for granted. And sold a pup.

Around this time I made another audacious decision. I would take my show to the heart of the Art Establishment but I would do it in a brand new fashion. So, I booked 28, Cork Street. A fantastic space in one of the most famous streets in London. I did this because I wanted to demonstrate that if you believe in yourself enough you can make your own history. You don't have to live your life on the sidelines. You can speak to

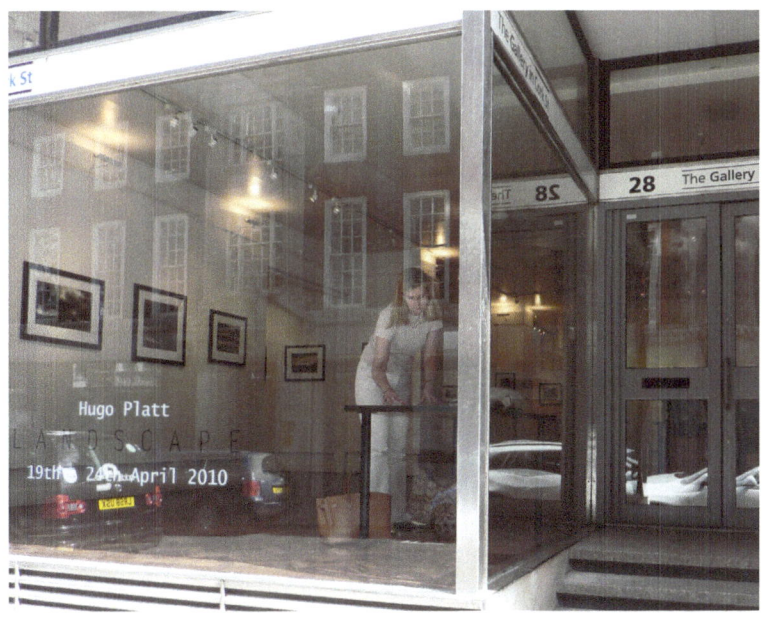

everybody – a global community and the traditional art world. You don't have to make a choice. You can reach out to everybody. I was also determined to change certain things about the way galleries work and the way Cork Street works. I wanted to revolutionise the way that art is sold and marketed. Instead of ordinary static shop fronts I would have a screen onto which the art would be projected, linked to various websites. Anyone, anywhere in the world could tune in. No one would be excluded. I would produce a book that took people by the hand. Anyone willing to give me a try would be taken by the hand. Instead of a price list with no pictures I would have a price list with pictures. A new sort of catalogue. I would link the exhibition to a brand – The Art Upstart. Me. And link it with the pre-publicity on Facebook, Twitter, Flickr etc. By the start of the show I would have built a global community of thousands. That was the plan. That is what I did.

The Art Upstart Twitter Community

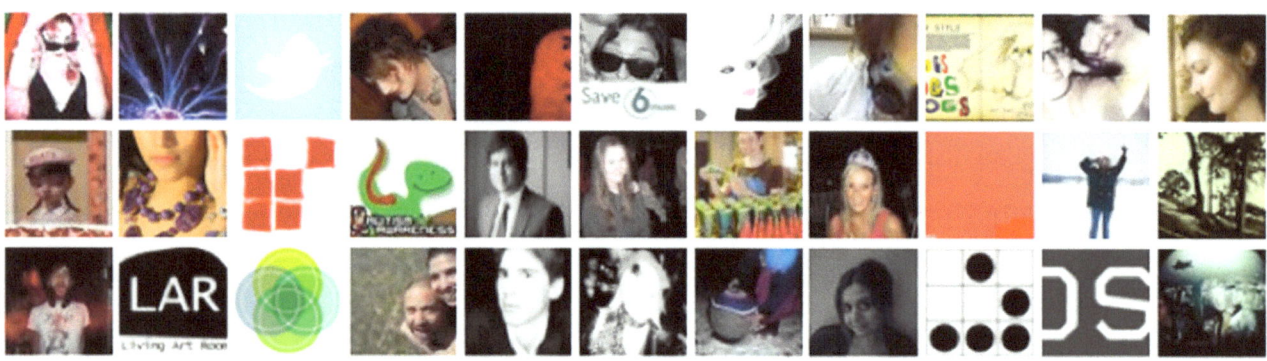

I had no money only a vision and belief. Interestingly as soon as I booked 28 Cork Street the doubters moved in. I asked a couple of art experts to join forces with me – both people who live in the traditional art world. They didn't like the idea that a nobody could stage a one man show – let alone in Cork Street. 'You?' 'Cork Street?' 'Surely not.' I asked one of them what they thought of my art. Answer 'I will tell you when I have spoken to someone else? I always knew I needed to have the judgement of the traditional art world – as well as our group of disparate followers. I don't disparage the people who know more about art than I will ever know. I was thrilled when a Mayfair gallery for whom I have a lot of time, asked me to approach a certain art consultant who would plug me in to the established order. She was a delight. She told me she loved my art. She told me she thought it was important. I was glad. Yet within 24 hours she flipped completely – 360 degrees. Like someone who was the victim of a protection racket, she called me a day after she told me I was something very special. She said, 'I can't act for you.' I asked why? She said because 'you are out of the mould. Too much out of the mould. My clients won't like it. You are attacking us. You are too challenging. You are too much of a revolutionary. I am sorry. I can't do it.' I said 'I am sorry. I was looking forward to working with you. I respect your viewpoint.' With that we ended. I never spoke to her again.

Enter the second Charles Denton. Charles is one of the most inspired and inspiring people I have ever encountered. He is the Chairman of the charitable Trust for Great Ormond Street Hospital, the children's hospital. He is a brilliant and a very spiritual man. Spectacularly successful at a very early age, he is as visionary as he is kindly.

I got to know Charles when I advised the hospital on various hospital PR issues. I instinctively liked him. I felt we were connected. We were both very driven. And both inclined to spirituality. Not everyone is. Anyway we talked.

Charles asked if he could see my portfolio. Once again I was apprehensive. I was delighted when he said he liked the work – a great deal. He would take me under his wing. A big wing. Once again, I was blessed.

Charles said he would think about the art world and how to launch a totally unknown commodity. I said I would do the same. We would begin not at the end but at the beginning. We would start with digital. Of course this was a risk. As far as I could tell – anecdotally – the art world was not really plugged into the digital universe or even to the internet.

One really big step in our thinking seems so obvious now. Charles said to deliver your vision you need resources – staff. You should hire some interns. Not just interns. Brilliant interns. Digital experts.

So I did. I sit on the Advisory Board of the Said Business School of Oxford University. The most dynamic part of a great institution. I advertised the vacancies on the Oxford website and, through College Hill, on the Bournemouth University website.

I offered each of the interns – three at first – a simple deal. They would work on the project without pay. They would be an integral part of the Art Upstart team. I would also train them in PR – providing tutorials on topics such as the capital markets, public policy, employee engagement. At the end of the three months I hoped they would get a job either in a digital agency or in PR.

The team was Sarah de Haas who had done a Research Degree in Oxford and was exceptionally knowledgeable about the workings of the digital space. She quickly emerged as the project leader. She was joined by Tasnia Wahid from Bournemouth University. And a couple of months later by Alessandra Durand and Ahmed Ashraf.

The initial idea was to create a following for the Art Upstart revealing my identity in the run up to the exhibition. Then the seeds of a bigger idea were sown. A friend said: 'Look, your art offers you a genuine opportunity to do something revolutionary.' 'What is that?' I asked. 'Well the work is very biographical and covers lots of historical events – right up to today. So, why don't you build an interactive art portfolio to run alongside the Art Upstart where everyone can join in.' I told him I thought it was an excellent idea – unique. 'I'll do it!' He told me that I would have to generate a lot of content. Writing as well as the paintings. I decided to keep the Art Upstart's identity hidden to evaluate whether people would respond to a truly and totally unknown artist. I started to write lots of blogs and Tweets about what I was trying to say in the work and about my experiences. I started to write a chronicle – in diary form – about my struggle to mount a one-man show. So the deed was done.

It probably helped that I love art but I don't love crap. A lot of contemporary art is crap. Installations immensely tedious – on the whole. I discovered very quickly that I was not alone. My early blogs generated a huge response.

Very quickly I discovered that there were an enormous number of people who are interested in art – who love it – but who feel disenfranchised – shut out. Their reaction was like my response to the Turner Prize. The people on the outside were often more interesting than the people on the inside. I was pleased to call myself the Art Upstart for this reason.

As I built up the 'posts' I came to appreciate that very many people – all over the world – are drawn to art. They may be artists or people with an opinion. A shift was also taking place. There was a new group on the scene. The online art community – knocking at the door.

The Art Upstart URL allowed users to tag my paintings with their own thoughts, connecting the work to real live people and events. The response was tremendous. Everyone was an art critic. Everyone had an opinion. The story of one unknown taking on the art world – attempting to break in from a standing start at the age of 58 – fired many people's imagination. The ups and downs gave the tale a ready-made drama.

As I got sucked in myself I started to take more and more risks – And learnt not to worry if I fell flat on my face. I just had to keep going. Cost continued to rise steeply. By the autumn of 2009, I had produced almost 70 paintings many of them very large. I could no longer house them all at home. They would have to be taken to a secure warehouse, labelled, wrapped and stored. But first I would have to take out an insurance policy the cost of which was eye watering. I asked Richard Selby to give me some advice. He believed I needed to cover the collection for at least a quarter of million pounds. A good round number! I contacted the insurance company. The quote was astronomic. In the end I took out a policy for £100,000 – which was costly enough. Then there was the gallery. I have put down a deposit of £1,100 in September but there would be two more payments of £3,300 plus VAT each one payable in March. The other in May. By now I had run out of money. In the summer I had taken delivery of a large batch of paints for £10,000. If I was serious and the show was really going to happen, I would have to put the whole thing onto a proper commercial basis. I would have to set up a company – with shareholders, income, tax deductable expenses. I had absorbed all my costs for the previous four years I could not keep going continuing to do so.

The next steps, taken in the run up to Christmas 2009 were both vital and critical.

First, a conversation with Charles Denton. I would have to lay my cards on the table. He is an extremely inspirational person. He would go on backing me. He would provide me with a loan to cover the cost of hiring the gallery. On the fateful day that this was decided, over lunch at my club, we agreed that I should set up a company, Art Upstart Limited. Any loans would be made to the company and paid off out of future sales. We talked about a lot of things that day. We talked about my book. I had decided to write a book to explain the emotional and spiritual journey I had embarked upon. I also wanted to explain what each of the paintings mean to me – the story. I didn't want to pre-determine people's response. To shut them out in any way. Only to explain what they meant to me. The more significant and important part is what the paintings say to the observer not the creator. However, I felt the audience may like to see whether there were any correlations between their own thoughts and mine.

We also talked about the need to have an offline strategy to complement the online. I was aware that a key part of the jigsaw would be getting an art consultant who could give us an honest opinion about the quality of the work, pricing and how to market the buyers.

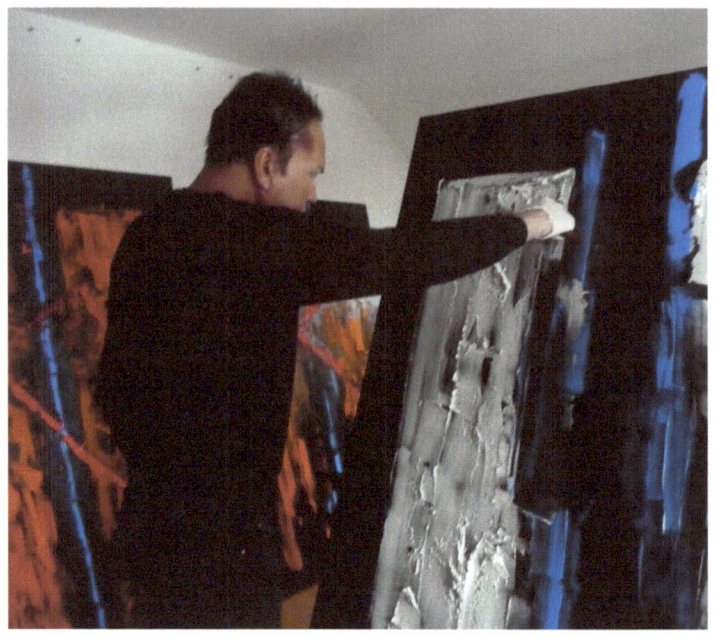

Over the Christmas break I worked non-stop. When I wasn't painting, I was writing. I took eight days annual leave from work to which I was entitled and painted the Blood series and Hell. Big subjects. Big paintings. I sent them to a few people who said they were fantastic. One of these people was a great friend who was to become the second investor, Richard Glynn. Like Charles, Richard is a big supporter of Great Ormond Street Hospital. In the New Year I approached Richard with the idea. I sent him a selection of my work and told him I needed help. By now costs were still rising faster. If I was going to meet the deadline, I would start having to get all of the paintings framed. Another very expensive task. I gave the go ahead. I would also have to be filmed doing the paintings for the website. Oh yes and interviews. There was no going back. I never thought of doing so.

After a period of two weeks – which seemed like an eternity Richard came back to me. 'They are remarkable. Fresh. Raw. I will back you. Would be delighted to do so.' So we cut a deal. As luck would have it, Richard knew an exceptionally talented art consultant who had worked for Christie's, Claire Bailey-Coombs. If she liked the work it would provide a tremendous boost. 'But be aware she will be very honest. If she doesn't like it she will say so. But if she does she is much respected and knows the art world very well.' Richard would help me set up the Art Upstart Limited. The tempo increased.

As we entered February 2010 the pace became frenetic. I had to decide how many paintings I should show at the exhibition and choose which ones. Not an easy task. I also had to decide which ones would sit side by side. With the great help of my wife I chose twenty eight. In the February half term, we booked the use of the school hall at the Vineyard School in Richmond. Jane and our framer, the ex-BBC cameraman,

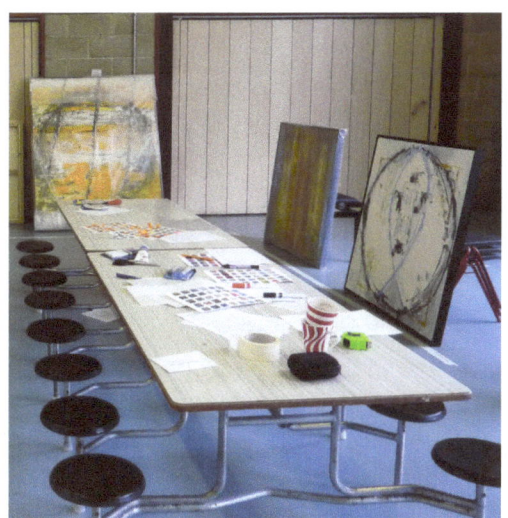

Alan Smith who has worked on the project from the start, hired a van and transported all the paintings to the school. They were joined by Justin de Deney, a professional photographer. I wanted to reshoot everything for the website. Jane and Alan mocked up the floor plan of the gallery using white tape. Once the photography was done, we selected each of the paintings that would be hung at the exhibition and grouped them

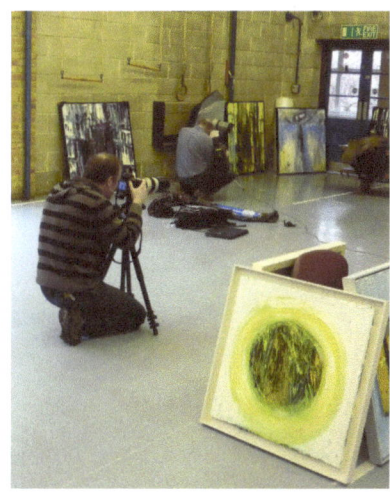
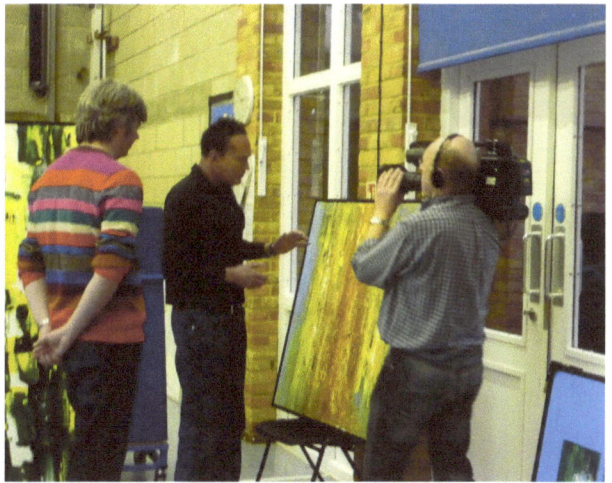

into batches that we felt worked well together. I did a few pieces to camera to explain what I was doing and talking about some of the paintings. Thanks to Jane and Alan we achieved a lot that day. When you undertake an exhibition you quickly learn that it is often a case of one step forward, two steps back. I tried to get a sponsor for the show during February but failed. The people I had in mind were already sponsoring an exhibition. I tried to get an up-market catering company on board – offering a sponsorship deal and failed. So two steps back. Then the big step forward.

Claire Bailey-Coombs came on board – fully and enthusiastically. Once again my wife and Alan played a vital part. And once again all the paintings had to be unwrapped and measured and their condition checked. Claire spent several hours viewing the paintings that day – a cold March day – in the flesh. I was at home with the flu. As the hours passed despite the fact I could not breathe and kept sneezing, I wondered how they were getting on. In many ways the biggest test so far. The most important day. At about 4.00pm I heard the key go in the front door and voices drifting up the stairs from the kitchen at the back of the house. I couldn't resist. I got dressed and went downstairs. 'This is Claire.' 'Hello.' Big smile. 'What do you think?' I asked. 'They are great.' 'Really?' 'Really and truly.' 'Would you be happy to work with me?' 'Yes. I would be delighted.' 'Seriously?' 'Seriously.' I was thrilled and hugely relieved. We would keep moving forwards. I explained about the book. I had already sent Claire some extracts. I told her it was going well. I asked her whether she would be happy to write the foreword for the book. I was aware that her endorsement in this way would add a lot of weight. She said that she would be honoured to do so. A great day. My flu got better quickly after that.

Towards the end of March – just before the Easter Bank Holiday weekend – I assembled the whole team. At the meeting I was told some very important news. The combined online following for the Art Upstart had just passed the 10,000 mark. The number of followers on Twitter was rising sharply. Better still I was interacting with people all over the world. The majority of my followers were based in the UK, USA, Canada, Germany. I was also building a following in countries like Switzerland, India, Spain, the Netherlands, Israel, South Egypt, Japan, China even Mauritius and Lichtenstein. Great news before Easter.

Over the Easter holiday I got to grips with the invitations to the exhibition. I had decided to sweat the asset. After all I would only get one shot at it. There was the book. Charles Denton loved it. 'I think the book is a page turner. I will publish it. I will be the publisher. The label Goodsteed.' I was relieved. I knew it would get published because I already had another person who had read the transcript and could see the potential. That said, there is no one in the world I would rather publish it. We were on.

At the meeting, Ahmed was a star. He understands fashion photography and Fashion PR. From the day I met him, I liked him a lot. He loved seeing us coming together as a team. A bit like a family. I was also blessed to have the services of Sarah de Haas and Alessandra Durand – both very talented, very passionate about art.

We talked a lot about the lists. Who would be invited when – on which days? The online piece was becoming more important. But first there was a big issue. The reveal. I decided the time had come for me to disclose my identity. I had built a substantial following. I wanted to thank them and let them know what I intended to do next. I mustn't delay. I must get on with it. So the virtual upstart linked up with the virtual James Hogan and in one leap with the real James. The impact was phenomenal. Suddenly all the people who had followed us – were engaged. They wanted to know more. They wanted to see who and what I am. They wanted to be part of the story. Suddenly the real world was connected to the World of Art to the Art Establishment via this thing we had created, The Art Upstart.

Along the way there were ups and downs. Not wanting to be sued for libel, on the Thursday before Easter, I visited a barrister to seek his advice. There were certain passages in my script that I wanted cleared. The truth is the most lethal, the most dangerous thing of all. On advice I edited two sections of my book. 'I'm sorry you have got a scoop.' He said – the barrister, 'but it is too dangerous, you could be sued. I decided not to risk being sued. Once bitten, twice shy and all of that. I left the meeting with a heavy heart, but a light step. It made sense. I returned to my office and kept on writing. By now I was totally addicted to recording everything.

Over the weekend – I worked. Worked. Worked. On the Sunday – Easter Sunday – I gave myself the day off – sort of. I had lunch with an artist – a dear friend and his lovely family. I told him what I was doing. He said, 'You always do what you say you will do.' He told me that he had recently walked through Mayfair and observed the closure of several galleries. We agreed the Art World was due for a revolution. Overdue.

I am counting down the days. Everyday there seems to be more decisions. No matter how hard I work there is always seems to be more work at the end of the day than at the beginning.

Today is all about lists and email addresses. The plan for the week of the show was decided weeks ago. I would open on Monday 7th June with a press preview.

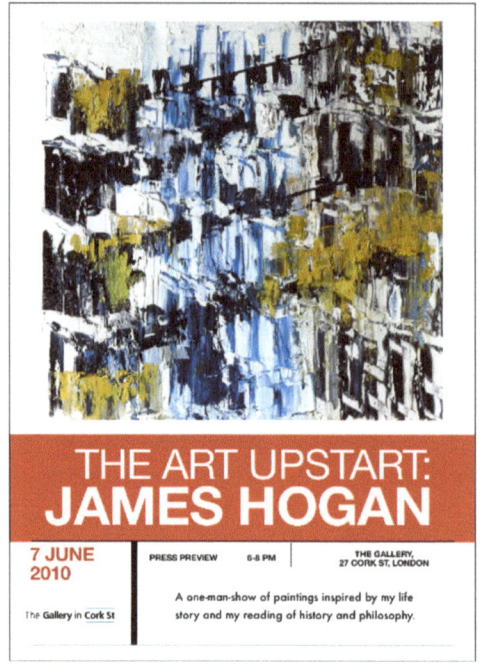

The opening night would take place on the following day. Thursday would be for corporates and the buyers of art for companies. Friday was yet to be planned. Open house day. By lunchtime Saturday 12 June it would be all over – A big success or a big flop. People keep asking me whether I am scared. Answer: 'No. I haven't got the time to be scared.'

So the lists. Monday night would be a risk because I don't know the Arts Correspondents. Maybe no one will turn up. I will have to get on the phone. I know many journalists on other parts of the papers – Business, City, Politics, and News etc. I will have to ask them for their help. The lists are very long. A big question. Who to ask for the opening night? It has to be the right mix of people. This is no ordinary event. There would be a lot at stake. I spent Bank Holiday Monday weighing up the invitations. Once I sent out the 'hold the date' I would be fully exposed as the Art Upstart. Already just before Easter my name was revealed on each of the social networking sites. There would be some kickback. I am a radical.

Meanwhile the book continued to make its own demands. On Bank Holiday Monday I had to select the family photographs to go into the Independent Spirit Chapter. We would get there. Early April – my wife and Claire travelled to the book designers and printers – in Norfolk – to make various decisions about the size and layout of the book. Everything suddenly fell into place. Everything became very real.

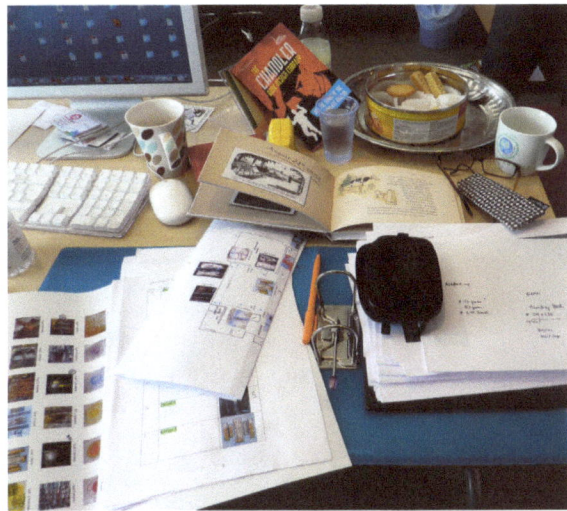

In the run up to the show I had promised myself – and Jane – that I would stop painting to concentrate on the arrangements. And cut down on the mess at home. In fact I couldn't stop. I painted **Void**. Then **Tramore.** A visualisation of a memory. The first picture I ever painted as a child. The first of the three 'Minus' numbers. The missing paintings from my childhood that got destroyed in the chaos that ensued. After my father died. I had come full circle. What happened next – at the exhibition – would be recorded history.

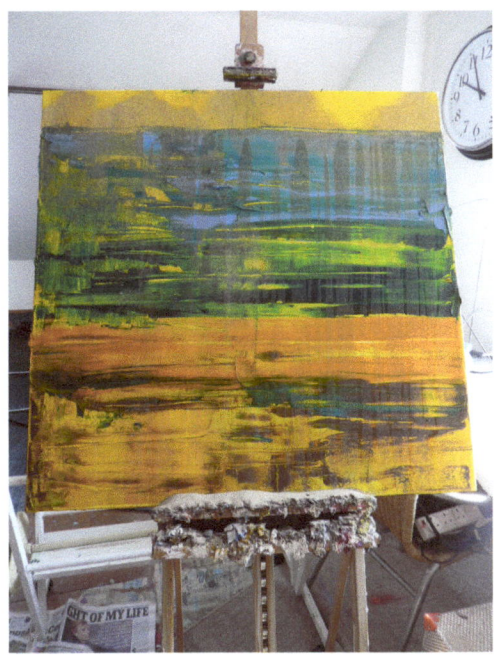

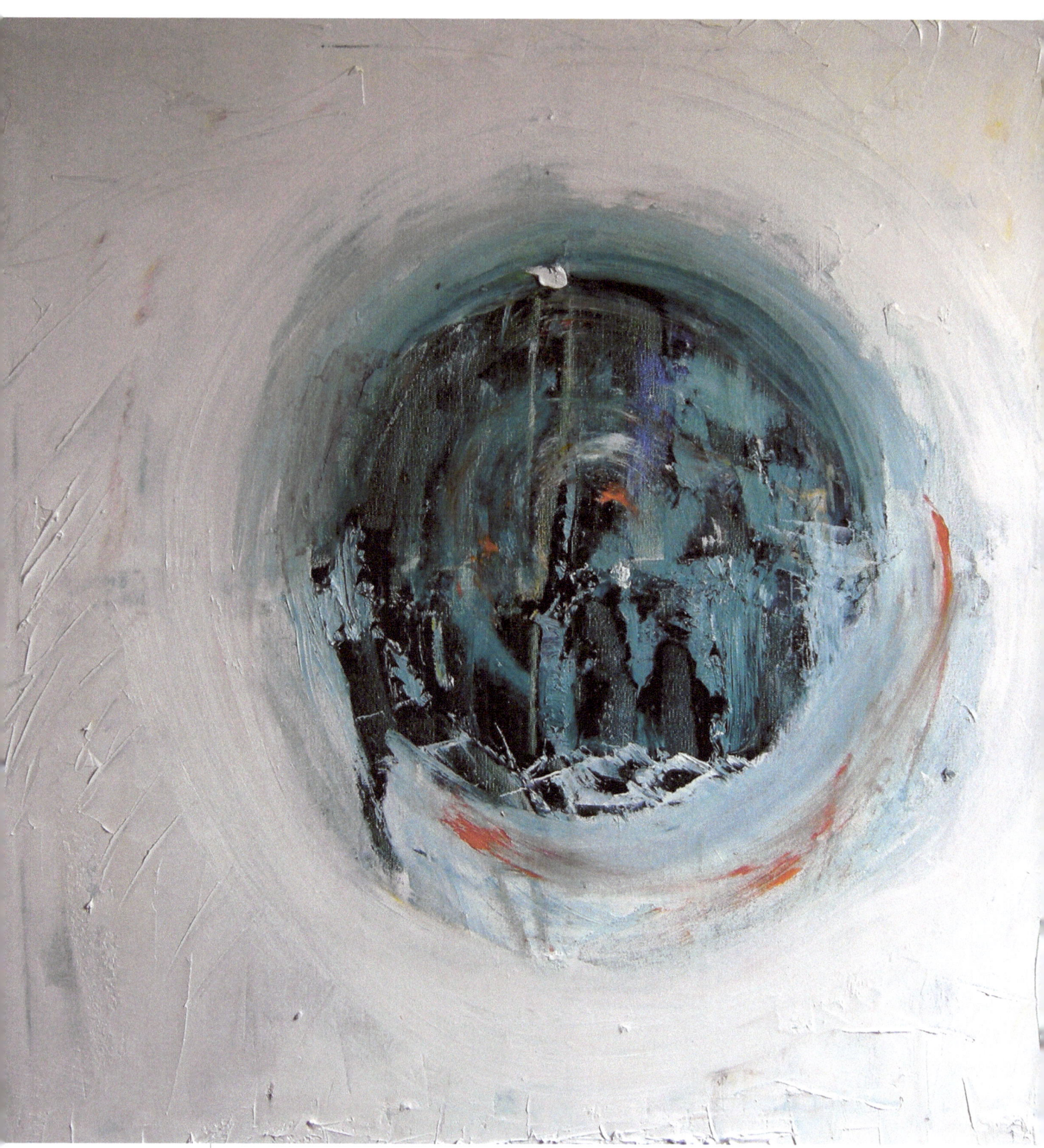

EMPATHY IV *2007*

THE WORKS

MPATHY IV: This painting introduces the idea of the undifferentiated mind in which man and nature, subject and object are wholly integrated. It evokes the warmth of the womb, and the psychology of unity. It invites you to travel deeper and deeper into the centre – never standing back. It asks you to reach over and touch. To feel the colours – the different greens of nature. To run your finger around the circle. To lick the outer rim working your way into the centre. The thickness of the colour gives security. Solace. The mix of different shades gives comfort, without challenging the centre of gravity. The blurring of the lines conveys warmth – the flicks of red heighten the glow. The reflections thrown off by the image give you the effect of inward looking through a lens or a sheet of glass – inviting you to peer in and get lost in an inner world. When I painted this image I thought about all the love that was shown me as a very young child. I thought about my parents – especially my mother – and the way that we lived inside a bubble – as a young family, as immigrants growing up in the 1950s. I thought also of my parents love of Nature, of the green, of Ireland. And the parklands in which we walked. I recalled the way it felt to inhabit such a cosy world – very green, very naïve, very innocent – an impossibly happy state.

This painting comes from a sub series in the overall story I wish to tell – there are seven empathy paintings in all. They follow the colours of the rainbow. The circle is used in this series because it is a complete form that is never broken. The lines of the circle embrace man and all of his emotions and sensibilities. This is both a child-like state and a pantheistic one. Everything is anchored in nature. The overall impression is in-ward looking. Your eye is taken into the centre relentlessly and only travels out to the

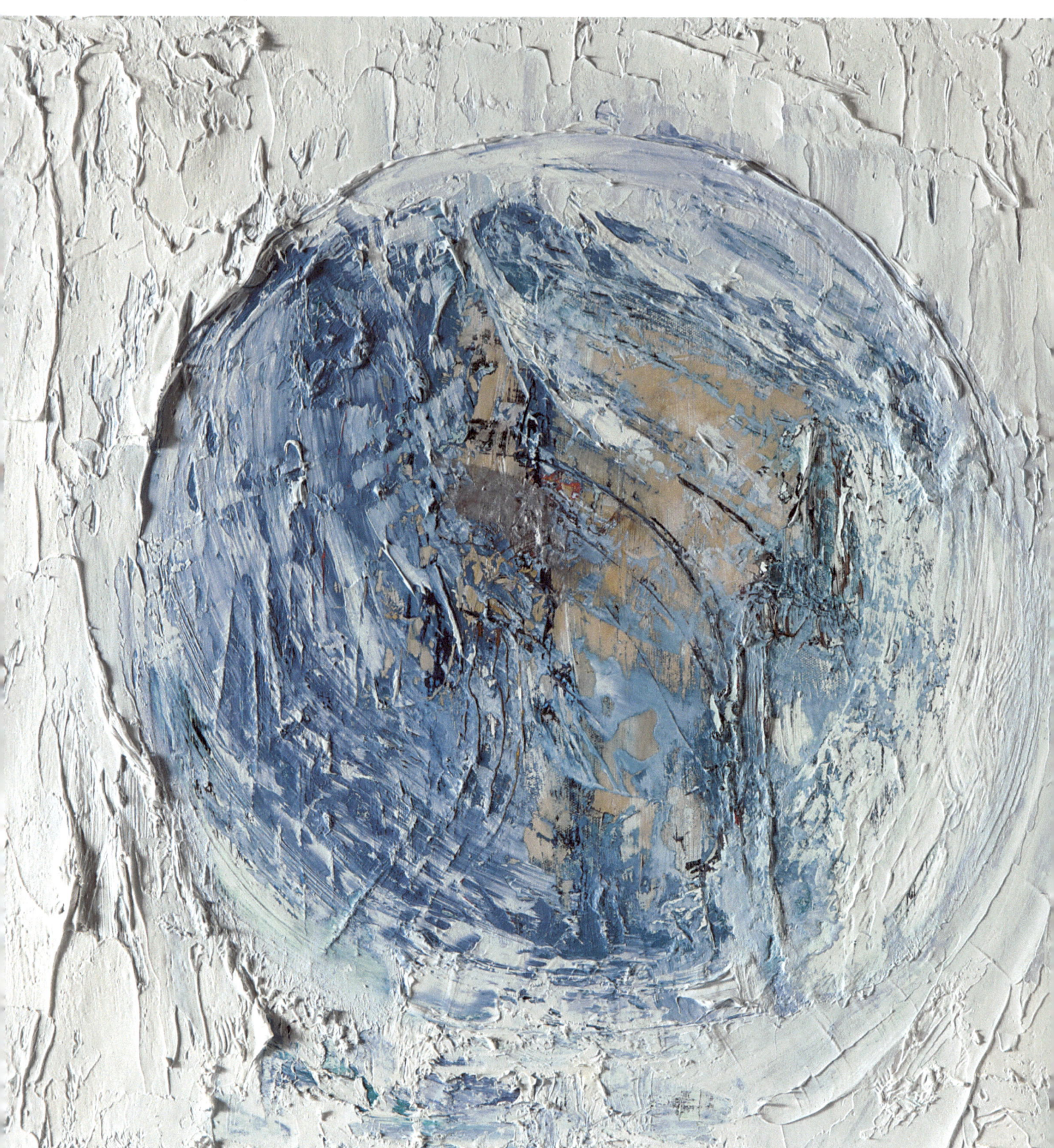

OPTIC I *2007*

inner ring of the circle. The use of thick white titanium is to invoke a mother's milk – thick and creamy and reassuring. The balm of unconditional love.

OPTIC I: When I painted this I felt as though I was taking a very personal and important step. Eyes are windows of the brain. The doors of perception. The idea behind this painting is an intellectual step and for every human being a very big emotional one. It denotes a stepping back. A degree of distantiation. The beginnings of separating subject and object. You stand at the foot of a staircase which will eventually push you out into the exterior world where you will become an independent spirit whether you like it or not. My feelings were intense when I painted this because I was so wrapped up in the state of Empathy that preceded it. I knew this would be a bittersweet moment. Coming to understand that there were other people in the world, other ways of relating, of seeing. But for me there was also the fact that by its nature optic focuses on the eye or the eye focuses on optic. Either way it was very uncomfortable.

My eyesight has always been an issue. I could look inwards very easily. It was looking out that was the problem. I also learnt around the time that optic became a development stage in my life – probably age 6 or 7 – that the way my eyes worked was different to most people. And that I saw differently. Around this age I became acutely aware of my abstract eye. My left eye is very lazy. I cannot read with it. I only see shapes, so as I looked out I became aware that something very mechanical was taking place. My right eye was empathetic with the world. And with my brain. It could cope with the looking out, beyond. My left eye, on the other hand, gave me a very insecure sense of the world when I looked just through that eye – it made me nervous of moving outside of myself. The mix was a very potent, troubling one. Ironically it gave me a faster route to alternative ways of seeing compared with most people. Certainly that is how it seemed to me. As a child – not really understanding what was going on – I repeatedly drew and painted pictures of the eye in which blocks of light illuminated the pupil like panes of glass or bits of steel.

This painting also reminded me of the virtual blindness I experienced when my right was patched. I felt a sense of terror when it was done. I instantly got terrible headaches and craved for the bits of light I could discern by peeping over the patch – inviting my good to illuminate the world. Weirdly, the effect of patching my good eye had the reverse effect of what was intended. By peeping over the patch

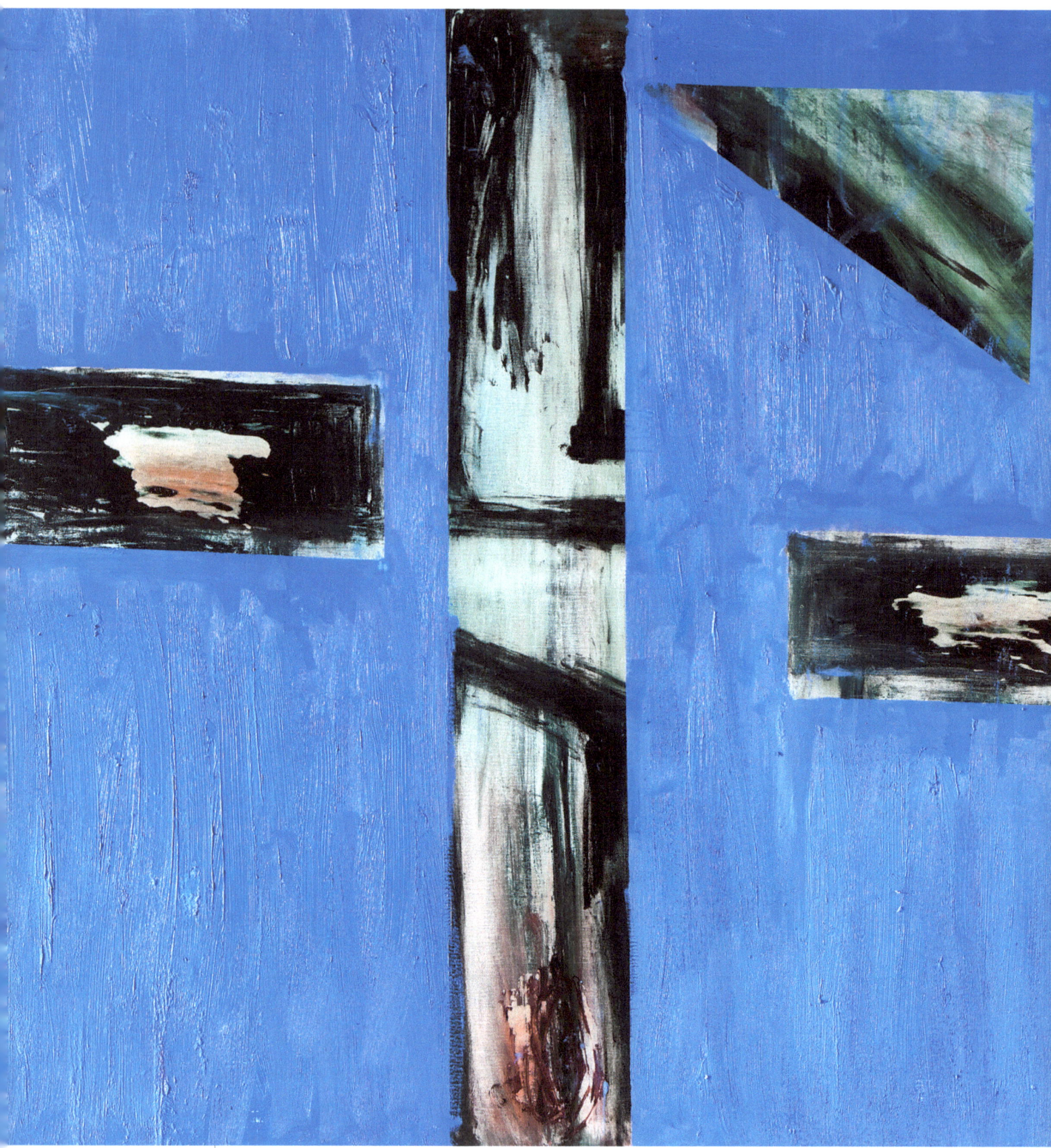

CHRIST IV *2008*

I actually started to use the good eye more – to look out, to start reflecting on my state of consciousness. My right eye was the physical manifestation and route to the intellectual state of optic.

Sight is by far the most important sense and sensibility. Beauty after all is in the eye of the beholder. So, for all its problematic nature, I wanted the Optics to be very beautiful. There are three optics in all – reflecting the right and left eye of man – and the spirituality or promise of a third eye. The Optics are also a pre-echo of Christ. They represent not only good but total perspective. The origin of being, historiography, cosmology – and so on.

The order of the Optics is also important when viewed from the outside. First the blue of the sea and the stars and the globe. Second, the green of the land. Third, the more refined lines and colours of Optic III denote a growing awareness of a life beyond.

As I did as a very young boy, I fussed and fretted over Optic I. I discarded my first attempt entirely. It was too cock sure. Too solid. It lacked insight and frailty. I wanted to share my feelings of uncertainty. I wanted the lines and the light to take us by the hand. I wanted to be optimistic – to share the experience of seeing beauty for the first time – but also to signal that such insight and ways of seeing come at a price. So the deconstruction of Empathy and the faltering awakening of a big more challenging world. The dancing together of colour and light across the canvas – the infinite variety of shades. The delicacy of fine lines. The fading away of contours only to return – to signal shape and shapes within shapes. Here then, ultimately, is a young child's eye.

CHRIST IV: I never had any doubt whatsoever that God exists. Of course it was ingrained in me. But I have always felt it.

At different points in my life my belief has carried me through. When people turned their back on me after my father's death, my belief in God helped me a great deal. I also tried to siphon some of that strength from me to my mother – like a spiritual transfusion. For many years it did not really work – she was too bereft – but by the time she herself came to die, she felt the same emotion that she'd given to me and now I gave back to her.

So the Christs. I did not plan them. I did not anticipate their arrival. I just went to bed, got up the next morning, and started to paint. And there they were. I didn't know

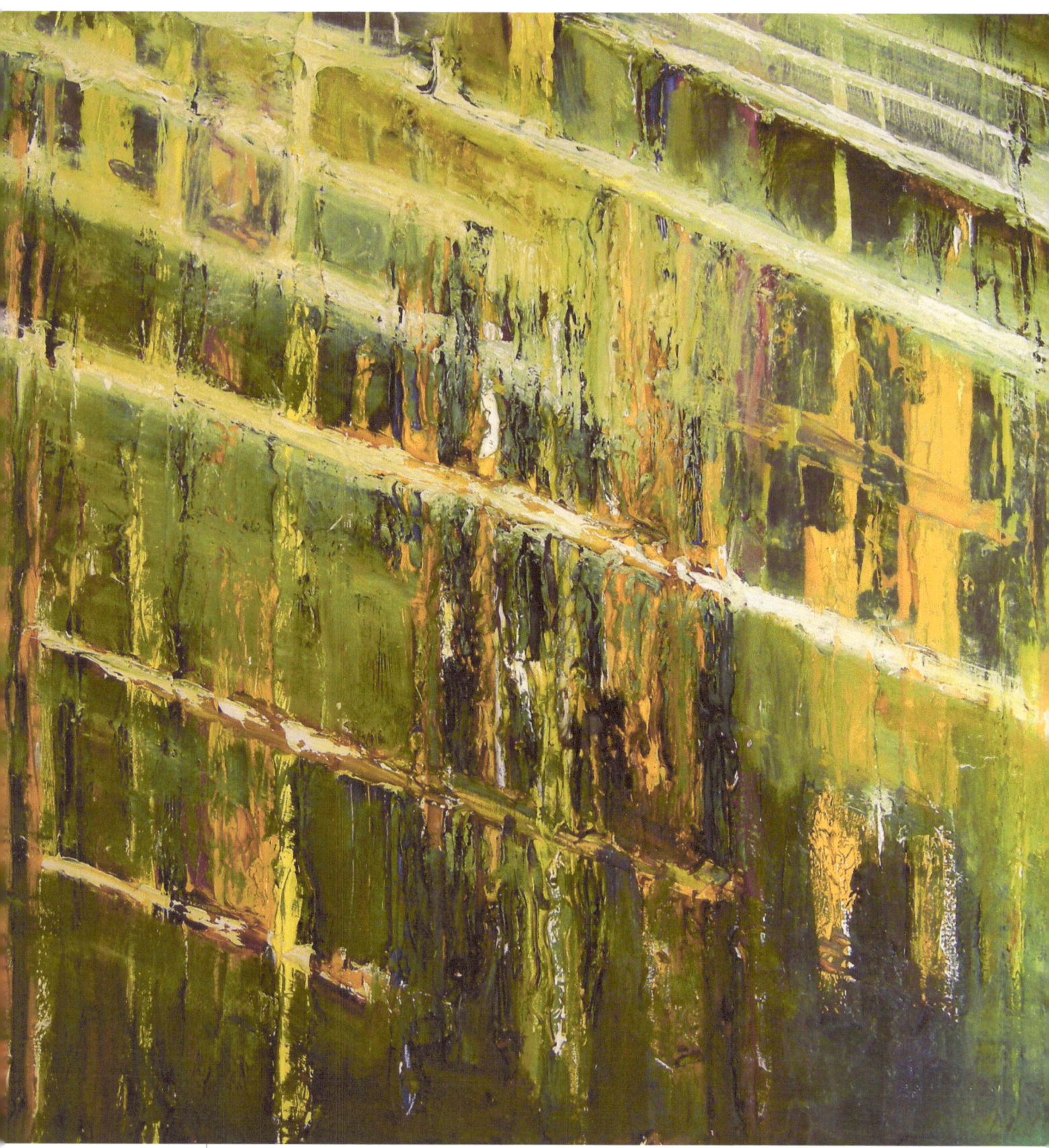

DIALECTIC I *2007*

that King's Blue Deep was the Blue of God, of Christ, of Good, in many cultures. I must have absorbed it. It seems obvious now. But not at the time.

When I started to paint them, it was as though someone else had control of the knife. A bit like Uri Geller. Some bit of magic. At first I didn't take a step back. I just did it. What I painted wasn't even obviously religious. Yet I felt an overwhelming sense of the existence of God in those paintings. When I did stand back – when I did allow myself to feel – I felt an overwhelming sense of the Holy.

They are the building blocks of Good against which Evil would rail throughout our lives. That's the easy bit. God versus man-made Evil. Later in my paintings I tackle this issue. But then there is the Hell that wasn't made by man – that's infinitely more difficult. Later still I try to address this issue also. Of course, I have no answers, only questions. I know what I feel. Beyond that it is impossible to resolve.

This picture depicts the assault on God. The attack from modernity, and its perverse consequences. Christ – which in my paintings is a universal symbol for good across different cultures and time zones – is deconstructed in the modern world but never defeated or eliminated. So it is here.

The backdrop of Kings Blue Deep, the colour of God/Christ, informs you that God is not subsumed. Yet, God is splintered. Separated out. Disjointed. In a way disoriented. The modern world has fractured our perception. Our understanding. In a certain sense, for a time, God is less able to fight back. The battle with Evil – with modernity and post-modernism – will intensify. And the threat – the attack – will get greater. But for now Christ – God – is hanging in there. Not defeated. Just threatened. This, of course, brings Him closer to humanity. Even God is allowed his weak moments.

When I found myself painting this image, it was hard to cope with – being a Catholic. Being a believer. I wasn't comfortable. But there was the paint. The God concept isn't easy. The imagery here has echoes of my childhood, evoking memories of my father being forced to work in an abottoir and the blood of cats whose throats were cut because no one could afford to keep them – as I looked on as a very young boy. As blood drains from the body – so too does life. As a young child looking on, I vividly recall the sight of great gobbets of blood flowing out of the factory where he used to work. And the current catching the blobs and blots of blood as they were carried downstream. This picture also reminds me of the houses I visited as a child in Southern Ireland where over the mantelpiece a picture of the bleeding heart of Jesus – pulsating red – was hung. Behind the bleeding heart, a yellow light offering hope.

DIALECTIC I: If you are an atheist the dialectic is a bigger idea than God. I am not an atheist. The dialectic in my paintings is both a beautifully framed construct – a bit like a mathematical formula applied to society – and a harsh reality – deterministic, deductive. In terms of the development of the collective consciousness, there is an inexorable tightening once man discovers the optic – the ability to stand back and judge. In my paintings the path to the dialectic is signposted by Reductio and Principia – both more narrowly defined but not yet a system.

The arrival of the dialectic, which in historical and intellectual terms came about with Marx and Hegel in the mid-19th century, is an earth shattering experience. In place of history there was to be a model – scientification and a route map. Economic determinism. Of course there would be light but its only source would be the inexorable logic and progress laid down by the dialectic. Or in other words the shade thrown off by the hard lines – the reflective and refracted light emanated by the heavy lines of an unbreakable theory. Thus the dialectic would take you by the hand – explain everything and all human endeavour – charting the highs and lows inside a perfect spectrum of perception and comprehension. In artistic terms the dialectic was both magnificently symmetrical and crushing.

When I painted the dialectic series – there are seven paintings in the set – I experienced all over again the excitement I felt when I studied dialectic theory at the age of eighteen at University. And, simultaneously, the hard-edged reality that arrived in my life the day my father died.

Of course the dialectic was the driving force of Communist ideology and the revolutionary theory that went with it, in its most distilled and perverted form in the Russian Revolution of 1917 and the Stalinist terror that took over following the death of Lenin. Apart from the huge loss of life the perversion lay in the fact that the dialectic was used to exclude possibilities – including art – rather than enlighten. Culture was subsumed by economic theory. Yet for all that the dialectic does throw light. It affords the ability to stand back, to analyse, to challenge the status quo – to see differently. The simple proposition that the historical process is the product of mixing thesis and anti-thesis to achieve synthesis is immensely powerful and illuminating, especially when it is separated from an exclusively economic analysis. My own experience of life between the ages of thirteen and eighteen referenced several of these insights. Life was desperately hard after my father died. I was presented with an inevitable outcome – yet I refused to accept it. I determined that my life would be more than the product of economic hardship. I lived somewhere between the hard lines of the dialectic and in the glow of its enlightenment. I understood my situation. And in that understanding I was able to find a path, another way. The dialectic is knowledge. Knowledge became my currency. I could trade my way out.

When I painted the first Dialectic, I felt the same excitement that I experienced when I first read about the dialectic. I felt that I was at the beginning of a new dawn. Yes the lines of the painting are heavy and thickly textured – to convey strength – but there is also great illumination. The yellows upbeat, the greens natural. Together they carry over some of the perception depicted in Empathy, albeit that the circle has been replaced with the stricter lines of the grid. The dialectic explains hierarchy and inter-relationships. So what is illustrated here is awakening.

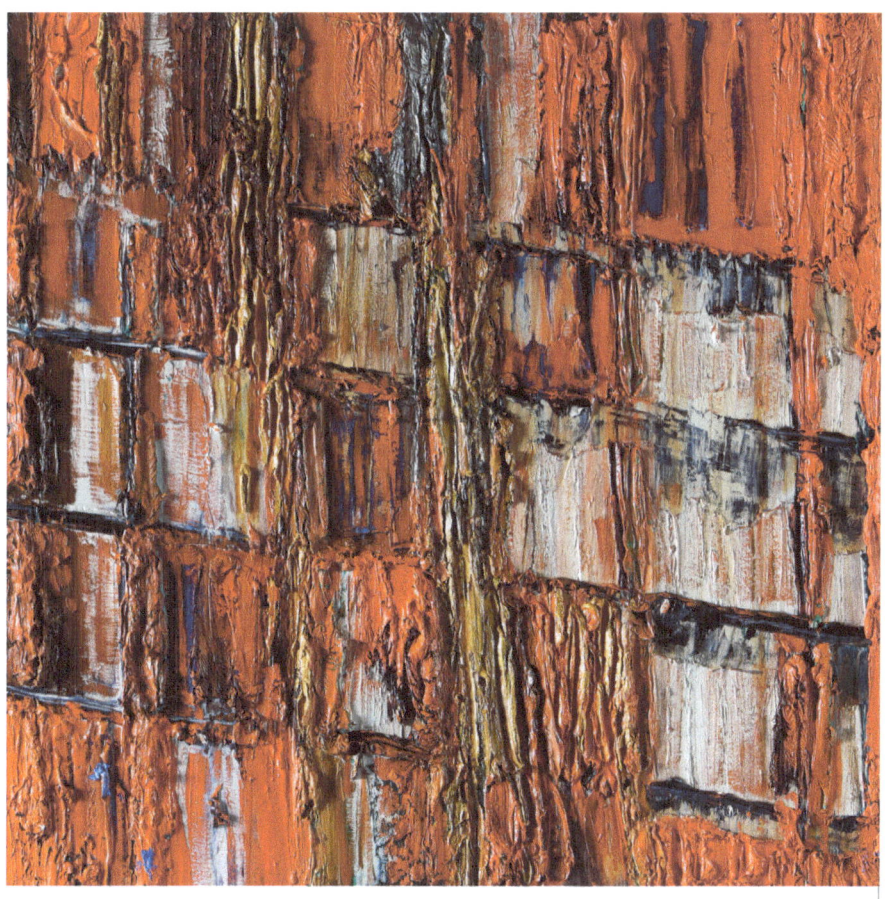

DIALECTIC III *2007*

120

DIALECTIC III: When I painted this I felt raw. I recalled some of the feelings I had after the age of thirteen when I was bereft and powerless. When circumstances were dictating a course to me to which I was implacably opposed. I used exceptionally heavy applications of the paint to convey the sense of oppression. I used the bloody orange to signal the forces which would attempt to suck away my lifeblood. Yet, as always with the dialectic there is light and shade – as well as dark. I used gold to define a certain optimism that would emerge from greater understanding, white to denote that out of the raw would come some good. The structure of the painting was executed to maximise an emotional response. The architectural style invites you to touch, to get involved. The white panels are illuminated in order to give even greater depth to the thick orange rectangles.

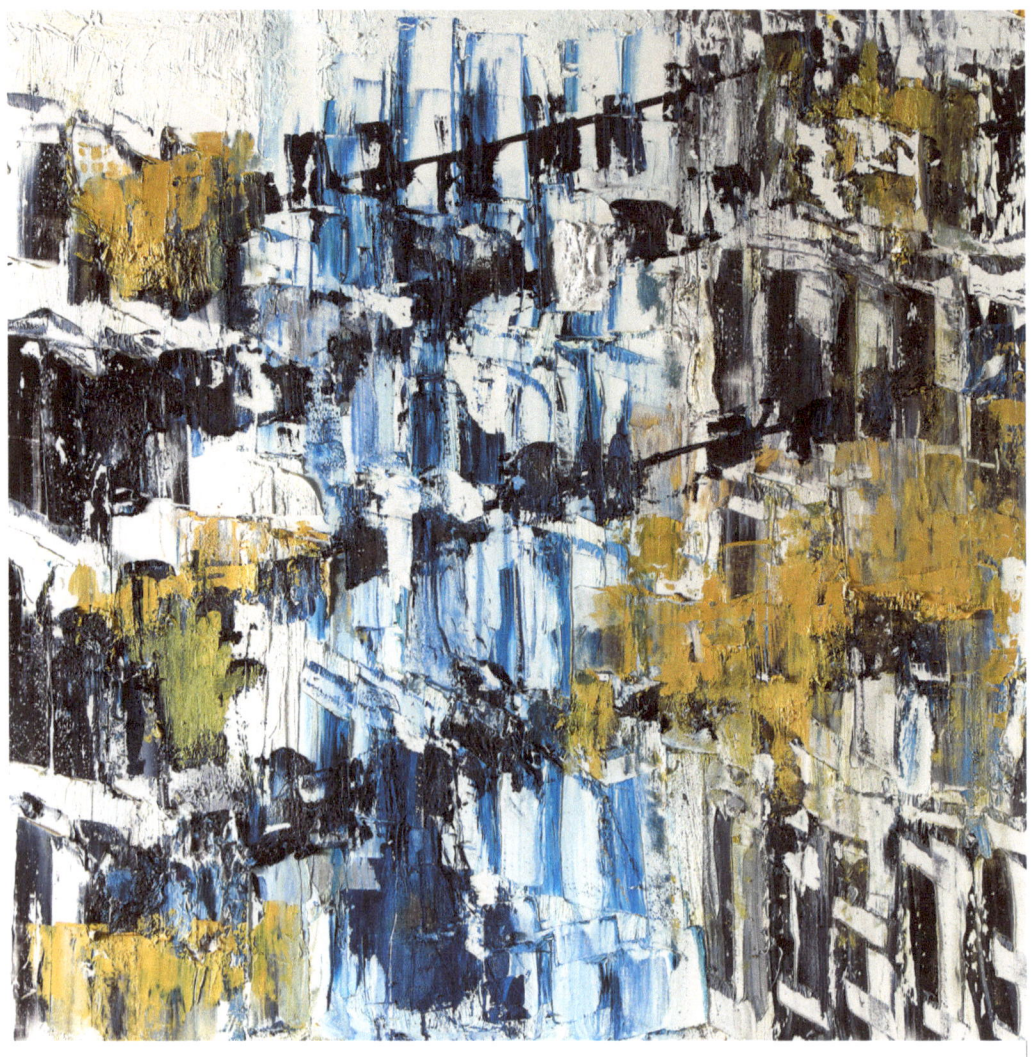

CRUCIAL IA *2008*

There is a certain brutality to it which is echoed in the later series of paintings which tackle Nazism, terror, and natural disaster, deploying a mixture of cadmium red and orange – wet on wet. There is blood lust in the dialectic as shown here.

CRUCIAL IA: is a link painting. It links the dialectic and its historical counterpart, anomie. Anomie is the sociological construct invented by Max Weber. It describes the break of society, of community. The deconstruction of the collective consciousness manifested in the atomisation of society. Hitler's Germany was an atomised society. Before he came to power, for a long time, the German people were refugees in their own country. Loners in a crowded room. Anchorless. Not knowing where they were or where they were going. There was no centre of gravity. No authority. No legitimacy. They lived in a vacuum. In stasis.

Crucial IA combines the certainty of the dialectic lines with the fractured lines of anomie. It is more existential in its feel and grasp. There are clear lines here but they are

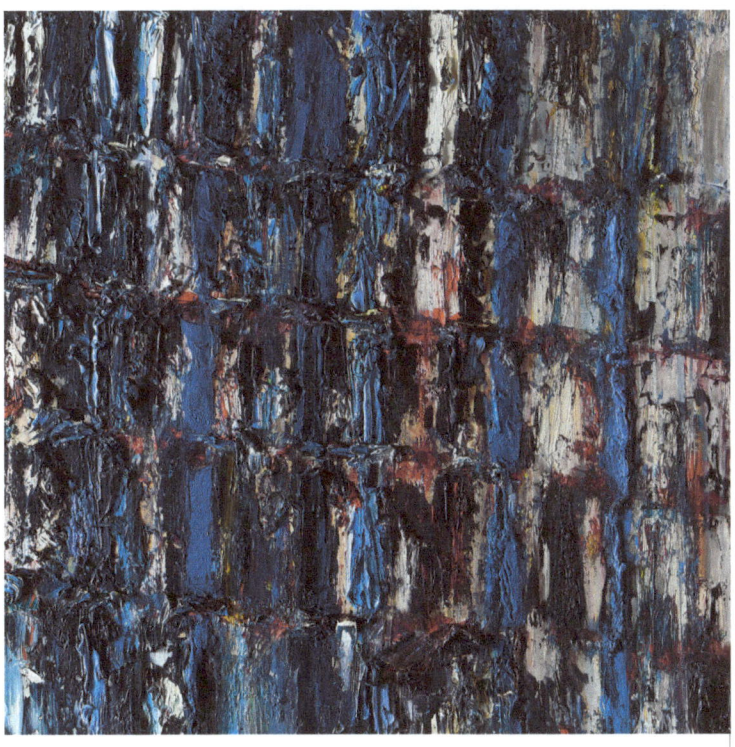

CRUCIAL I *2008*

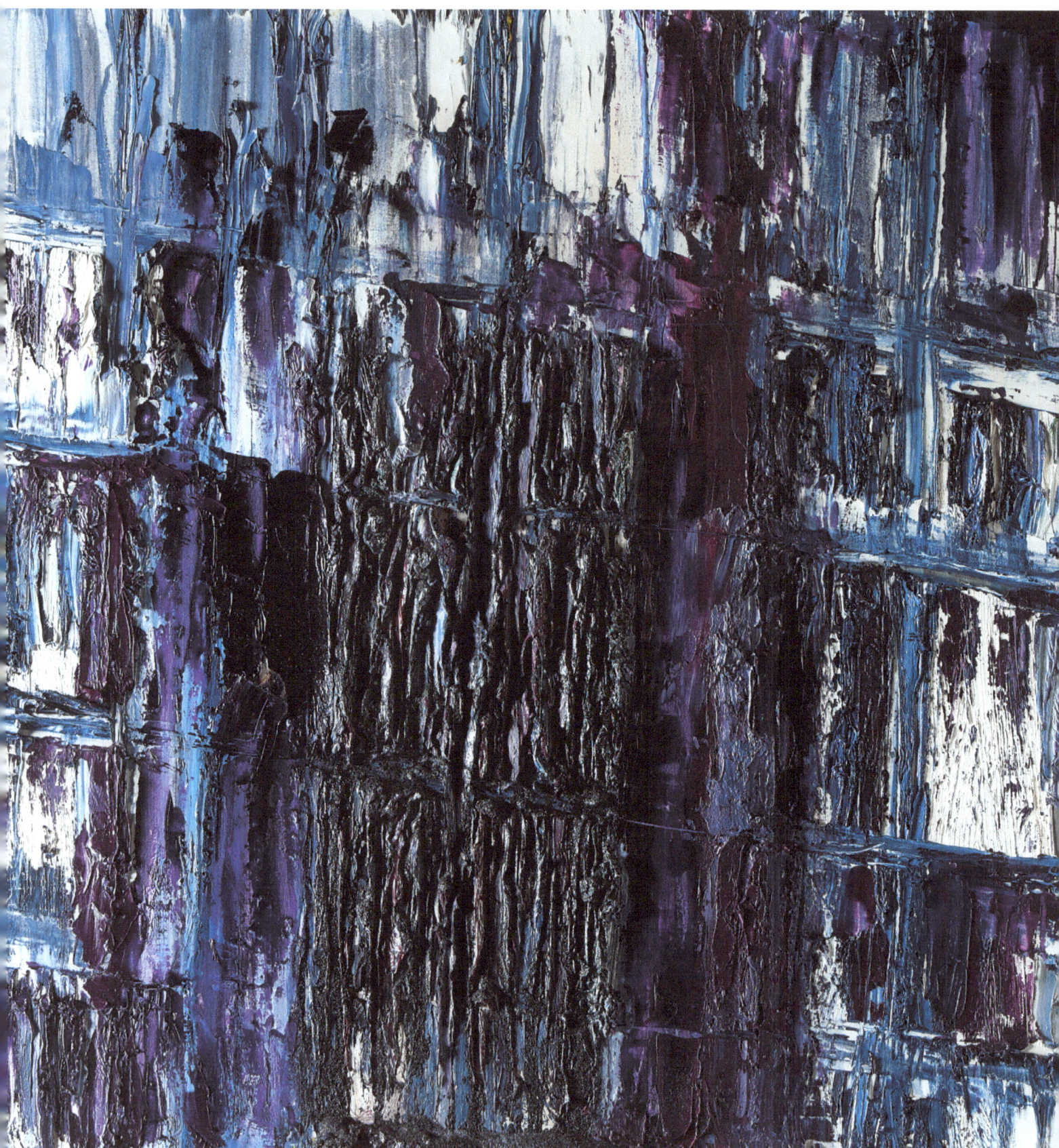

DIALECTIC VI *2007*

being broken down – eroded. It is not all bad, however, as society loosens up so there is more scope for freedom of expression and experimentation. This duality is represented in the combination of thin black lines and waves – a bit like what you would see on a heart monitor – and the white spaces populated by scrapings of gold. In my life I experienced the anomic society in microcosm. The loss of my charismatic father left us all as free as birds and desperately detached.

CRUCIAL I: takes you deeper in the anomic psyche – adding strength to the idea and complexity of form. When I painted this I took my mind back forty years to the way we lived when I was a teenager. The anchor of the family had gone. So too the anchor of the Catholic Church. In lots of ways my mother died when my father died. She found his death inexplicable. As with natural disasters, her question was, "Why? Why do that? Where was God that day?" Her faith was shattered. So there was a double – even triple bereavement. The loss of our leader. The loss of our mother. The loss of faith.

This painting also extends the upside of the anomic state of mind. It is at its heart an existential sensibility. I have always been attracted to that. And as I painted this picture I recalled the liberation that came along with being bereft as a teenager. Christ never left me. Nor does he in this painting. The challenges to which my faith was exposed are reflected in the myriad of blues. The baby blue of Christ is present but there are a wide variety of blues to capture. The shifting sands around me at that time in my life then connects with this idea. The use of yellow across the piece is also to connect with the dawning of a new state of being that is by no means all bad. The dark patches are there to take you into a lost world but also to throw into relief the benefits of the struggle – the gain. As the first fully fledged painting in the Crucial series the painting has been composed to draw you in – take you down a tunnel – taking you to safety away from the flames of hell.

DIALECTIC VI: When I painted this I focused on beauty and complexity. The dialectic is as complex as it is simple. I used seven different shades of violet to convey this. On top of that I wanted to add great depth and texture, in keeping with the concept.

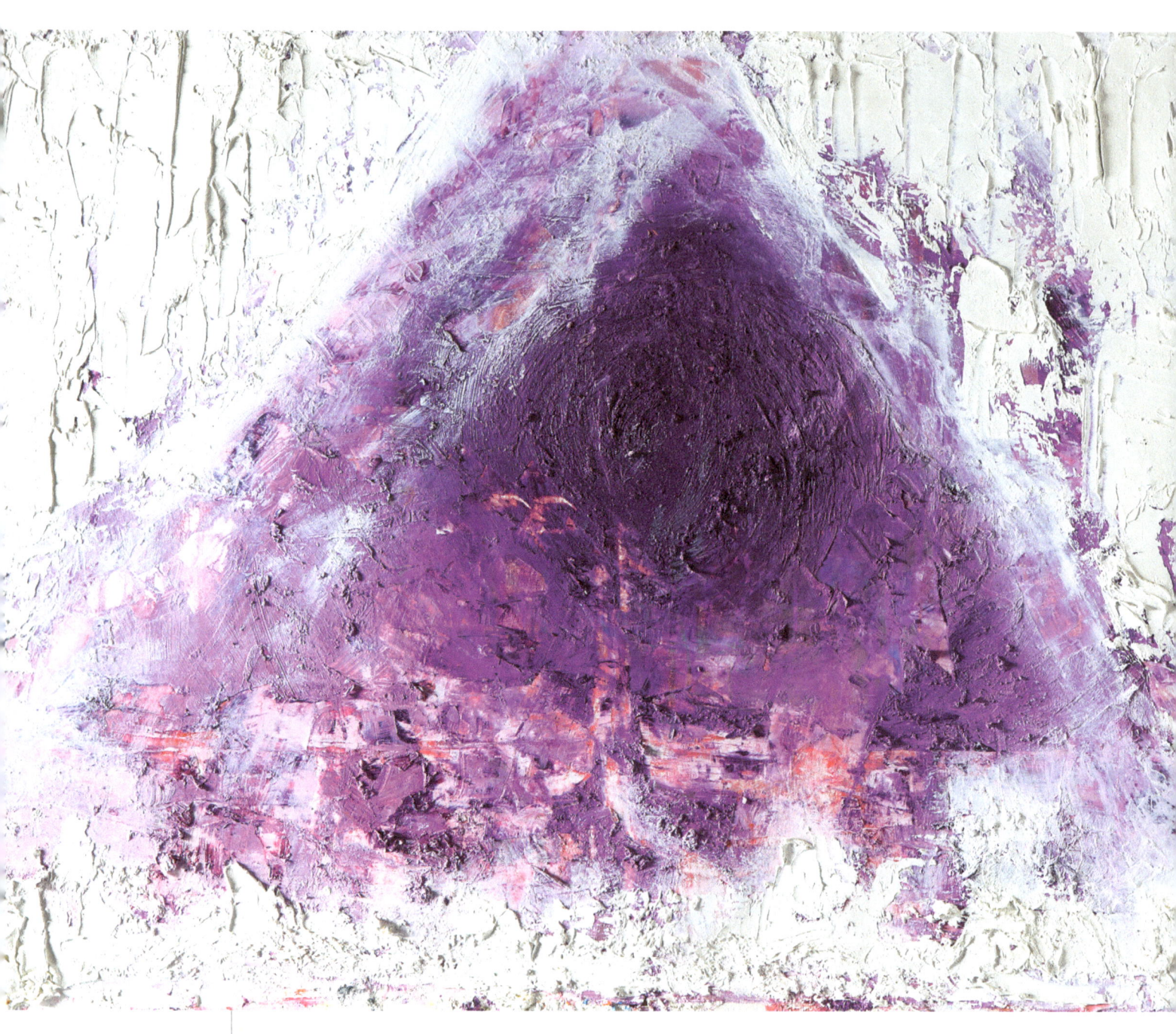

STRANGERS IX *2009*

So I layered violet upon violet. Varnish upon varnish: yacht varnish. I felt emotional when I painted it so I want to show my emotion, and get others to embrace it. I wanted to say all the things I needed to say about the dialectic – a difficult concept – but to express it in a beautiful way. In a sense this painting showed me that I could say very difficult things in an aesthetically pleasing way. And be accessible.

I chose the circle, the grid, the rectangle, because we are all human beings and these are the shapes of childhood. By using them, I hoped to open up my thoughts and feelings to a wide audience. In doing so, to share and release the emotion I felt at the time of doing them.

STRANGERS IX: In historical and philosophical terms Strangers depicts the alienated consciousness described by various writers including Marx and Hegel – and people like Jean Paul Sartre. It is a symptom of the dysfunctional society, of disenfranchisement. Minorities and counter-cultural groups are familiar with the feelings evoked here. As I painted this painting I relived the feelings of marginality and of living on the edge that I experienced in my teenage years. In those years there was very little structure in the way we as a family experienced the world. We were forced onto the sidelines, by circumstance. We existed on the margins of society. We had to define ourselves entirely. As a result I became very self-aware. Very sensitive to the way I perceived the world and the way others treated me. I developed a scale of ambition. A psychology of challenge. I acquired a taste for my own space. A certain autonomy. I became a very independent person.

When I painted this I wanted to recreate the different aspects of this phenomena – good and bad. I decided to take the triangle because it's beautiful and simple. Behind this picture lies a lot of mixed emotions and a difficult idea. I wanted to convey the fact that you can be a stranger in your own land and in your own head – and benefit from the feeling, the ecstasy that comes with the awareness. In order to get across the notion of marginality – of counter-culture – I decided to corrupt the lines of the triangle and to create confusion by blurring the field of vision. I wanted to pull you into the centre of the triangle and push you away at the same time. I began with a circle of purple – continuing the use of the rainbow – and spread it out into the misty contours of the deconstructed shape. As with the dialectic which uses this colour, there are many different shades of violet used here, layer upon layer.

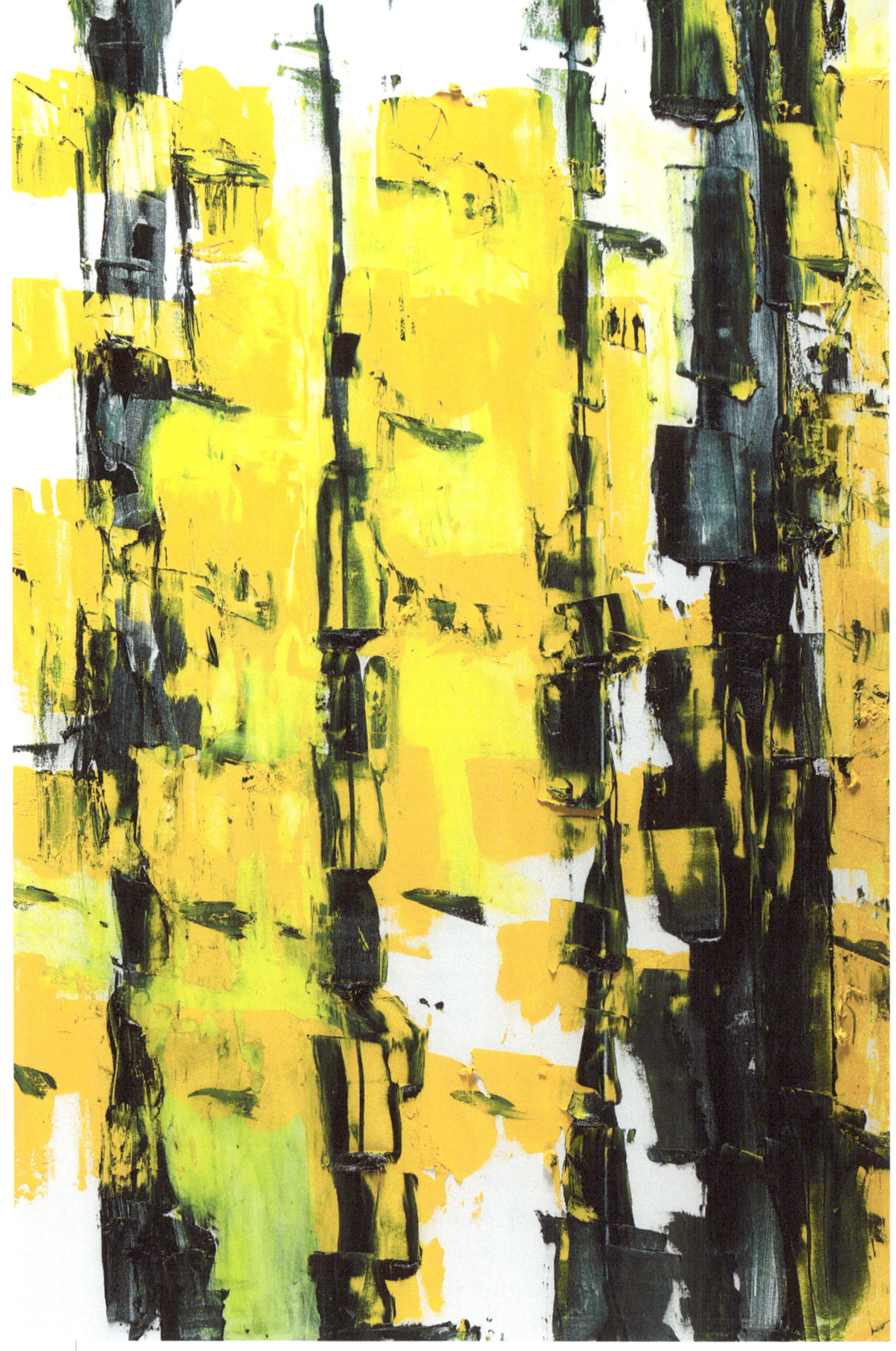

DILEMMA II *2009*

DILEMMA II: This painting has a simple purpose. I wanted to draw together the dialectic, anomic and alienated forms and in doing so to provide a punctuation mark. I also wished to distill an essence. When I commenced the work I didn't know whether it would turn out to be a dark representation – too intense – or whether it would be bright. I didn't plan the colours. They chose themselves – perhaps because I didn't want the end product to be depressing. I experimented with the sap green – which I used in the Empathy series – And was pleased that it allowed me to make strong and darkish lines without being oppressive or to blocky. I used the different yellows for a similar reason. I could define the shapes I needed but let your eye through deeper and deeper into the picture without being too intense. The overall effect was paradoxical. Here is the dilemma. I have taken three potent symbols of three very potent ideas – combined and mixed them together on the canvases and ended up with a relatively calm and peaceful painting – naturalistic in feel. I think this happened because of the way I have interpreted these concepts. Yes they can be dark and foreboding but they are also sources of light and enlightenment.

Although God is not directly referenced here His influence is present in the optimism that lies behind the dawn light evoked here. Reading left to right, the first column reflects the blocks of the dialectic albeit that the certainty of the grid is starting to break. The middle columns, 2 & 3, represent the more fluid imagery of the anomic. There are blocks but fewer of them. Column 4 on the right hand side is closest to the alienated consciousness in which not only the sap green lines are blurred but the greens and yellows flow into each other.

Ultimately the message is one of hope.

ECLIPSE VI: This painting represents the head on clash of the two most powerful symbols of good and evil in the history of the world – Christ versus Nazi. When I constructed it I wanted to convey the immense power of the Nazi brand at its height and the deep-seated fear that it instilled. I used a mix of cadmium reds and black to echo the colours used by the Nazis and give the impression of different types of blood. Some streams of blood. Some thick blobs. Some emanating from open arteries. Some the dried blood of the dead or dying. I layered different tones of red upon the cadmium in order to suck you in and invite you to see behind the brand, into the depravity that lies beyond. I created a bloodied eye intended to draw you down a tunnel and then

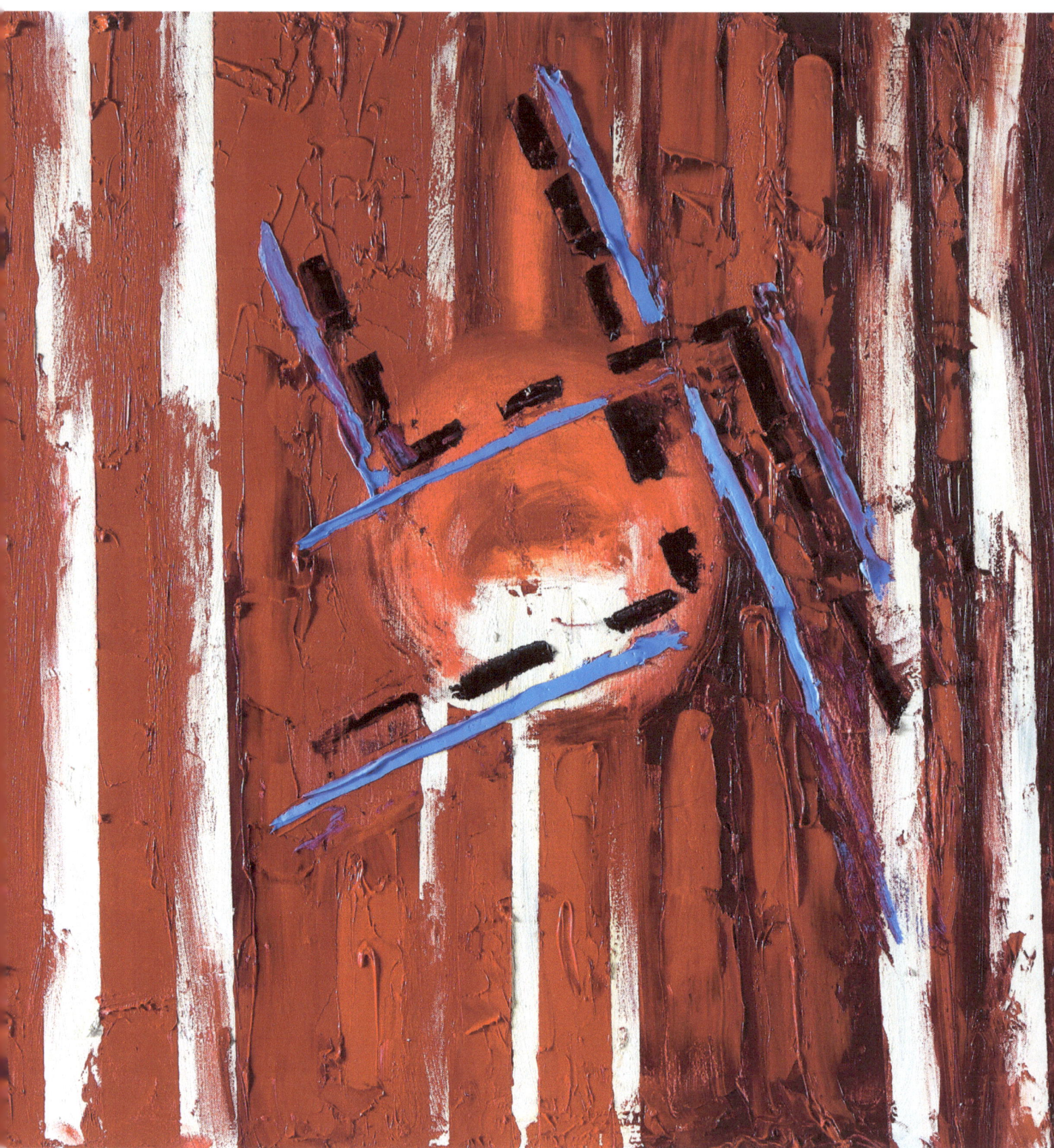

ECLIPSE VI *2009*

push you back to the total field. Against this backdrop the Christ fights. Despite the overwhelming power of the Nazi imagery and its potency at its height – the Christ causes the splintering and deconstruction of the swastika. The lines of the swastika are broken – fragmented: the shape is maintained but its impact is lessened. At its extremity – on the left hand side – its mark is almost erased, certainly sketchy. The lines of the Christ, however, are strong when measured against the broken lines of the swastika.

When I painted this a flood of memories and emotions came into my head and onto the knife. I remembered the racial hatred. That deep-seated fear that it would crush everything in its way. The destruction. I also felt the love of God. The non-servum of the Christ. The refusal to give up or give in. The physicality of the struggle. I recalled reading Paradise Lost/Regained in which the devil has the best lines – the most powerful symbolic imagery – and yet loses in the end.

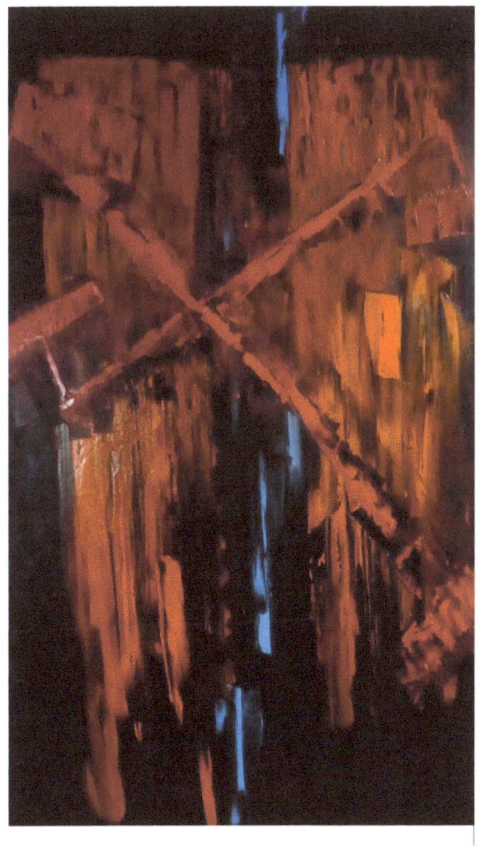

BLOOD II *2010*

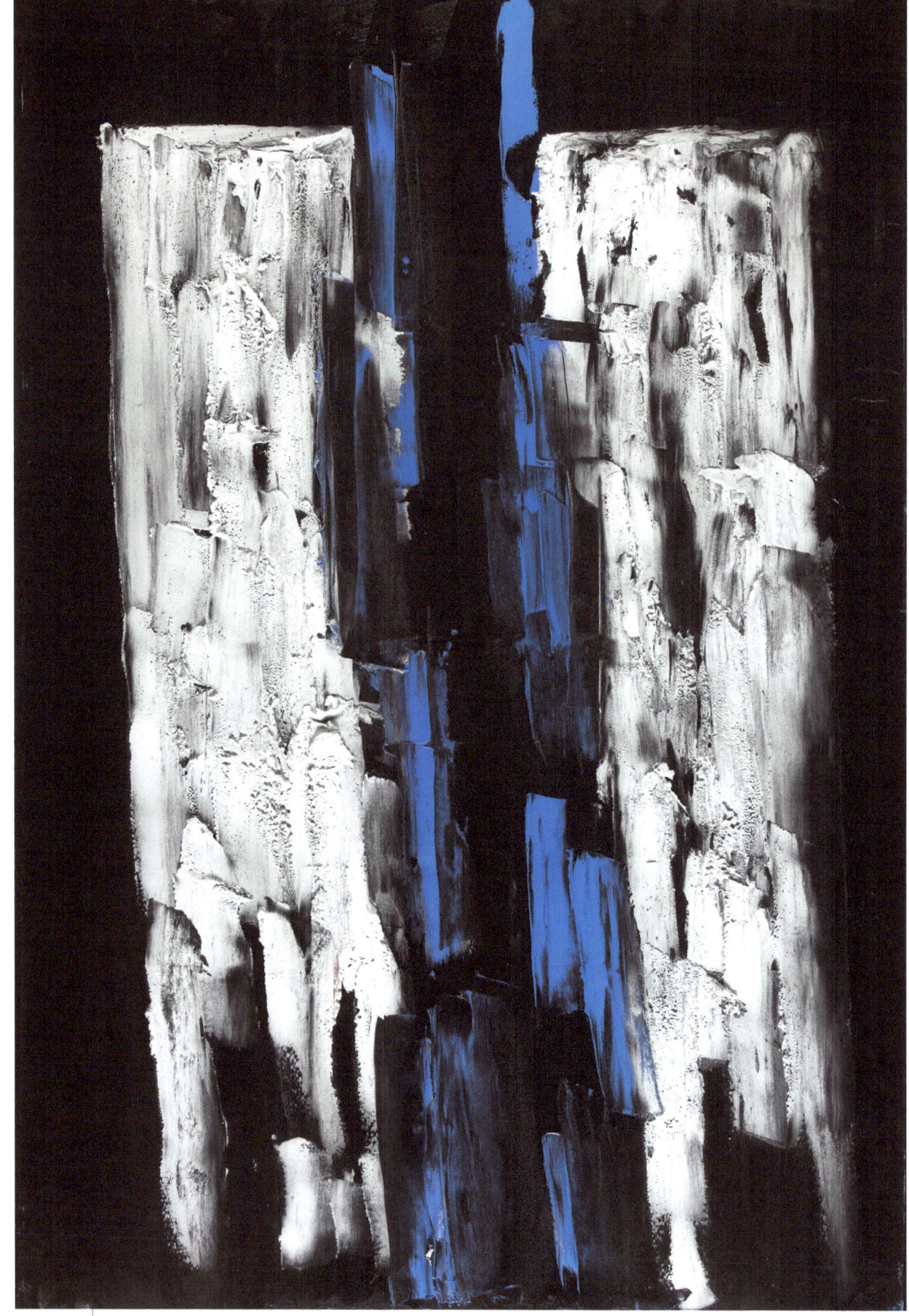

BLOOD III *2010*

BLOOD II: When I painted this picture I relived the horror I experienced along with the rest of the world when Al Qaeda ripped into the Twin Towers. I recalled the day of the attack. The bloody violent eruption. The slaughter of the innocent. The sick celebration of the perpetrators. I remembered also visiting Ground Zero. The scale of it. The obliteration. I re-lived standing on the roof of the Empire State building and looking out to the enormous gap in the skyline where once stood the twin towers – where once lived and worked so many people. Now rubbed out. Gone forever.

As I layered the paint I dwelt on the fact that this was a man-made disaster. But there was no symbol. Just anonymity. The hidden hand slitting people's throats – Al Qaeda. But I wanted to expose it. To attribute blame. To depict the struggle. So I invented a fabled symbol of evil – an abstract construct – mixing ideological imagery which bites into the towers, ripping it to shreds. I chose to mix different reds and oranges in a thick paste to provide depth and shed light upon the bloody stains. I wanted to set the towers afire in order to distill the evil presence I felt. Against this depth of black echoing the descent into hell. And the glimmer of blue – of Christ – that lingers, threatened, but present.

BLOOD III: When I painted this picture, I wanted to move the imagery on from the first in the series. A little bit of time has passed. The twin towers are now ash. There is greater clarity. The beginning of the realisation of what has occurred – the simple horror of it all. The design. The perfect crime. After the bloody deluge – silence. Vacuum. There are no burning bodies only cinders. The towers are crumbling. They will collapse. As they fall, the Christ starts to emerge stronger. A sign of hope. A source of reflecting light. The blue takes you by the hand. It filters the dark. Allows you to see through to the other side. As I painted it I felt less anger. A sort of calm descended on me. I felt the towers collapsing. At the same time I felt the air would clear. That there would be the chance to move on. The bottom 20% of the painting is important because you get the impression that the whole edifice will fall imminently – but not the blue. The blue has no structure. No construct. It exists in mid-air. It is eternal. Ironically, I found the imagery comforting. No longer grotesque. No longer terrifying. The event is what it is. The painting is what it is. There is no panic. Man did it. Man will do it again.

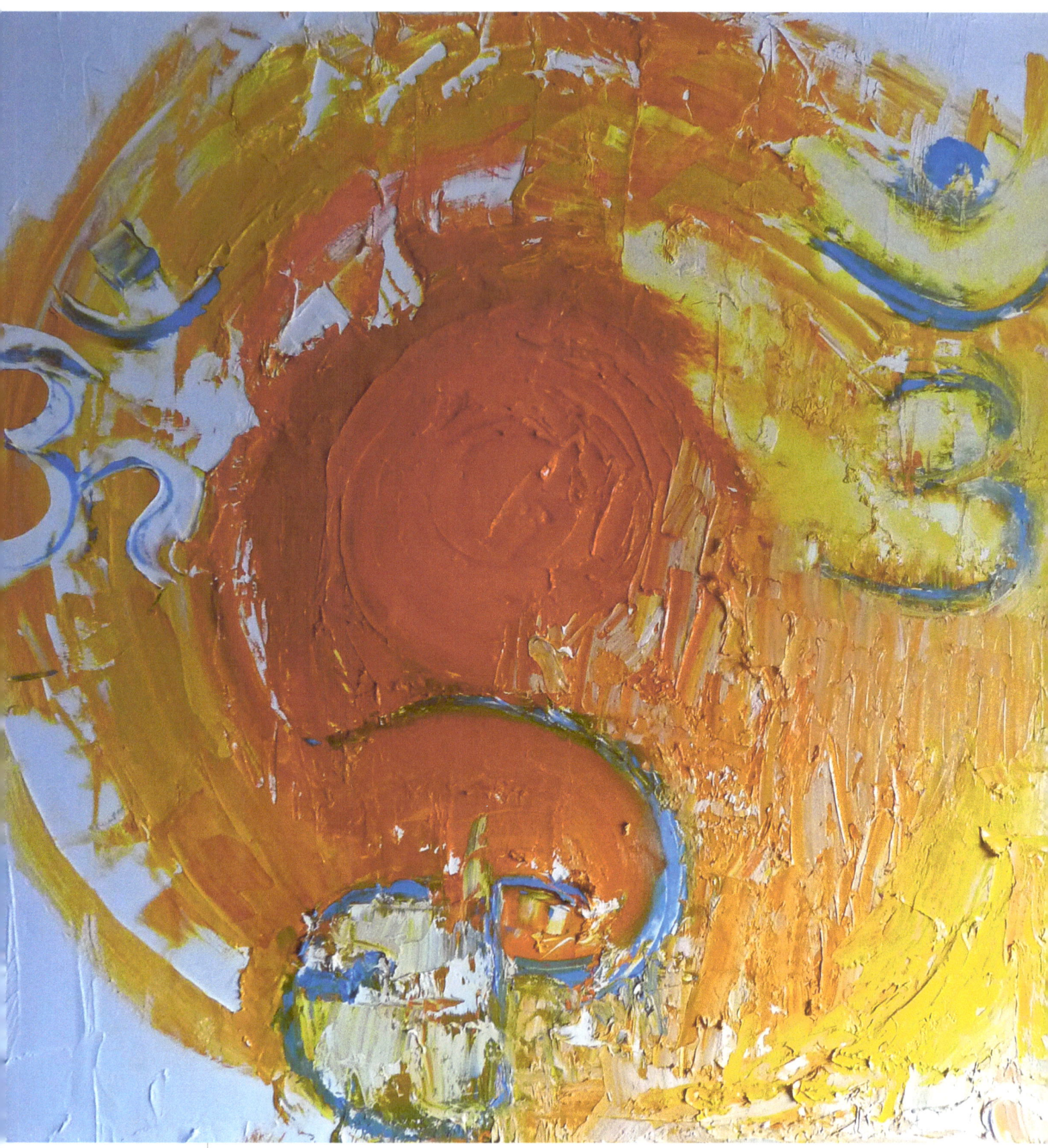

ASHOK *2010*

BLOOD IV *(see page 14)***:** This painting is in effect a detail of the larger Blood in which the Twin Towers are depicted as ashen blocks. It is saying the same thing. The reason I painted it was to give an extra perspective. Also my mind needed to dwell on the imagery and colour created in the first painting of this type. I also wanted to show the strengthening of the Christ as the towers disintegrate.

ASHOK: This painting was a labour of love. I painted it for a very dear friend of mine a Hindu, Ashok Tanna. Ashok is a very kind, very gentle, very spiritual person. We drew out the painting together because I wanted to be sure that the symbols were sympathetic to each other to the eye of a Hindu. I also wanted guidance about the colours. I mixed the colours on the canvas. However, Michael Harding does not make terracotta – the base colour in Hindu art – so I made it up. Also the different yellows and oranges. I painted the symbols in blue because of its religions significance in my work. Yet even here I let the blue blend into the authentic Hindu colour. I was nervous about how Ashok would react to the final product because it was outside of my frame of reference. I was delighted when he told me he was very pleased with it. Since I finished it – in March 2010 – I have left it on the easel and returned to look at it several times. I have observed it changing with the changing of the light throughout the day. It instils calm. Which is the effect I wanted.

When I look back over the last four years, I feel extraordinarily lucky and privileged. As I progressed with the work, I gathered a lot of people around me who showed me great kindness and gave me a lot of support. They always encouraged me. They never said 'you can't do it'. Others did but not my close circle of friends and supporters. I came to realise that they would not let me fall or fail. They would put their arms around me and catch me if I faltered.

I am now looking ahead to the new chapter of the paintings – the next 75. I hope my theme will play to my strengths and help me to say some important things. I have always been fascinated by counter-cultural imagery and ideas. And by the fact that beneath the official history of mainstream society was another very different way of seeing. I have already chosen many of the colours I plan to use. And started to re-research the 50s and 60s. Reminding myself about the people, imagery and way of life of the people I studied as a young man. I am very excited about this next step, keen to get going all over again.

INDEX OF PAINTINGS

INDEX OF PAINTINGS (continued)

The following images reproduced with the kind permission of :

Roxy Matta
Principia

Marcello Nucci
Crucial I

Alex Sandberg
Empathy IV

Ashok Tanna
Ashok

Rob Woodward
Empathy VI